Habit Driven Weight Loss

Over 60 Surprisingly Simple Habits to Transform Your Body and Mind

Todd Hoff

Weight Control is a Habit, Not a Goal

> **You do not rise to the level of your goals. You fall to the level of your systems.** — James Clear

This is a quote from the multi-million best-selling book *Atomic Habits*. It's one of the big ideas in Clear's book.

What does it mean? Here's my summary:

- A **habit** is a regular practice or routine.
- A **goal** is a result you want to achieve.
- A **system of habits** is the collection of habits leading you to your desired results.
- You will improve the likelihood of **controlling your weight** by creating a system of habits.

- To succeed, don't focus on your weight; **focus on the habits** that control your weight.
- It's your habits that **decide your future**, not your goals.

This message obviously resonated with a lot of readers. You don't sell millions of books by accident.

Here's the Problem with Other Habit Books

They don't tell you **what habits** will help you control your weight!

That's where this book comes in. I've lost over one hundred pounds and kept it off for 20 years.

That's rare. Really rare. Was I on some magic diet? Was I on some magical exercise plan? Am I somehow special? No, no, and definitely not.

What I did was create a system of habits that helped me lose weight and maintain my weight over decades. That's what I mean by *weight control*. Weight control isn't about becoming supermodel thin; it's about your ability to maintain your goal weight range—forever.

Since we are going to be discussing the phrase *system of habits* a lot, let's be clear about what it means in this book:

A system of habits is a combination of habits that work harmoniously together to naturally bring about the outcome of weight control—without having to rely on willpower, starvation diets, or crazy workout routines.

Is that what you want? Here's what you need to do...

Create Your Own System of Habits

You are already a success. You come from a long line of ancestors who survived many torturous periods of famine.

You are also among the first generation with complete responsibility for controlling your weight. You can't rely on your environment to make you exercise, you can't rely on your environment to limit the calories you eat, and you can't rely on your environment to make you eat the right things. If you want to exercise more, you must find a way to make it happen. If you want to eat the right, you must find a way to make it happen.

It's a big responsibility. How do you do it?

I'm sharing with you my weight-control habits and a process for creating a system of habits, so you can create your own weight-control system.

The habits shared in this book will help you recreate your world, so you can finally bring your weight under control.

Will your habits be the same as mine? Many of them. But your life is different from mine, so your system of habits will evolve and take its own unique shape.

What's invaluable in this book is that you learn two things:

- How to create your personalized habit system.
- Habits that have already been proven to work.

How does my system work?

Minimizing Slip-Ups

You **slip-up** is when you eat more or exercise less than you intend. All it takes is a few slip-ups a week to gain weight.

Consider this: 200 extra calories a day, one lousy extra soda or candy bar a day, can make you gain 20 pounds a year. Now imagine what happens when slip-ups add up over decades. Obesity is what happens. That's all it takes to edge into obesity: just one slip-up a day.

That's why you can't rely on willpower. One slip-up is nothing, but they add up over time.

Have you ever lost weight only to gain it back again? You likely did it one slip-up at a time. That's why this book is about weight control, not just weight loss. Learning a weight control system is how you prevent what seems like the inevitability of regaining all that weight.

How do you prevent slip-ups? By creating a system of habits that reduces the probability of slip-ups to as close to zero as possible.

Over time, more and more of our lives slip under our conscious awareness until one day, we wake up and find we are living on automatic pilot. Many of the habits in this book are about reversing that process and bringing your actions back under your conscious control.

Building a system creates a protected bubble where you naturally achieve your goals without relying on willpower every minute of every day.

There are habits for every vital part of your life: personal, home and family, activity, food, car, shopping, work, school, and community.

The habits systematically remove slip-up opportunities from every area of your life. Minimizing slip-ups maximizes your chances of controlling your weight for the rest of your life, and that's what this book is all about.

It's Like Baby-Proofing a Home

A good way of thinking about creating your system of habits is that it's like baby-proofing a home.

Baby-proofing aims to remove any threat that could hurt a baby. Likewise, the goal of your habit system is to remove any threat that could cause you to slip up and lose control of your weight.

When baby-proofing a home, think like a baby and remove every possible way a baby might hurt itself.

When creating weight-control habits, **imagine** every possible slip-up that might cause you to lose control of your weight, then create habits to minimize those potential sources of failure.

How do you go about baby-proofing? You don't put up post-it notes asking your baby to please not touch the power outlets. You don't have a heart-to-heart talk to tell your baby not to go near the stairs.

Why? Because babies don't understand.

In the same way, your body doesn't understand that it's no longer 25,000 years ago, and not every food commercial means it's time to eat, and you aren't going to starve if you don't eat for a few hours.

Walk into your kitchen. Imagine all the ways you can slip up and lose control. Open the refrigerator. Are a few goodies hidden away? Toss them. Don't have goodies in the house—ever. This habit reduces temptation because you can't eat those extra calories if they are not in the house.

Repeat this process in every situation where you might lose control of your weight.

Pay attention to your life, identify what might be dangerous, and remove the danger. Look for any forces that might cause you to slip up, and neutralize them with habits.

You can't change your genes or the world in which you live, but you can use the same incredible human qualities that made the modern world—your ability to think, learn, grow, and adapt—to create habits in which you have no choice but to succeed.

How to Create a Habit

This book isn't about habits in general—it's about **you** building a system of habits that will help **you** control **your** weight for the rest of **your** life.

That's what I want. That's what you want. That's what we all want.

So I'm not going to go into detail about habits. I'm going to assume you've read other books on the subject. But I don't want to ignore the topic altogether. I'll summarize the process from Atomic Habits, as it seems straightforward and research-based.

Create a good habit in four steps:

1. **Make it obvious**. To remember your habit, make it obvious so you'll do it.
2. **Make it attractive**. Combine a habit you want to practice with something you love doing.
3. **Make it easy**. Make tasks small so you can't say no.
4. **Make it satisfying**. Add immediate rewards to reinforce a habit.

That's how you create a habit.

Do you want to break a habit? Do the opposite: make it invisible; make it unattractive; make it difficult; make it unsatisfying.

Naturally, the next question is: what habits should you adopt? That's what the rest of this book is about. Let's get started!

Wait, I have a surprise for you! Be sure to read to the end; there's a free offer exclusively for readers of this book.

1. Habit: Create Your Own Habits

Throughout this book, we will cover a lot of potential habits for you to consider adopting. Some are short and simple. Some are complex and involved. All can be powerful forces for controlling your weight for the rest of your life.

Don't stop with my list. Create your own list. There are two general strategies for creating new habits:

1. Borrowing Habits
2. Inventing Habits

The goal of this habit is to create your personal *Habits to Try* list. This is a list of all the potential habits you'd like to audition as part of your personalized system of habits for weight control.

As you find new habits, add them to this list.

Now we need to solve a problem: where do you get new habits from?

Borrowing Habits

New habits can be found anywhere and everywhere: books, friends, TikTok, Instagram, Facebook, YouTube, and podcasts are just a few sources where habits can be found.

There are a lot of bright, creative people out there with new ideas you might never think of on your own.

Keep an open mind. When you come across an interesting idea, think, does that habit make sense for me and my life? If it does, add it to your Habits to Try list.

Inventing Habits

You can also invent your own habits. To create new habits, you have to be able to imagine how your life could be different. Your future has yet to be invented. It could be completely different, and the way it changes is one habit at a time.

I want you to mentally time-travel through today, tomorrow, next week, next month, and next year. Imagine your life. Go slow. Go into great detail.

While picturing your life, imagine what changes you could make in your life to make it better. What are you proud of? What are you not so proud of? What do you wish was different?

Try seeing your life from the eyes of a stranger. What would they think? What advice might they have for you?

Try flipping your life on its head. Imagine doing the opposite of whatever you are doing now.

Now imagine your life with those changes. Play through all the different scenarios in your mind. In each scenario, your life could be dramatically different than it is today. How does it feel?

Take any changes you want to incorporate into your life and add them to your Habits to Try list.

Integrating New Habits

Get in the habit of searching for new habits to adopt. Once you start looking, you'll find them everywhere. When you find one, add it to your list.

Now you have a list filled with exciting potential new habits to adopt. How will you integrate them into your life?

That's what the next habit—*Daily Check-in*—is all about.

2. Habit: Daily Check-in

This is a simple, clear, powerful step-by-step process for weight control.

When do we learn the process for controlling our weight? We don't. What we learn are marketing slogans like "eat less and exercise more."

It's worse than useless. It's frustrating and demeaning and makes you want to give up.

The secret is learning how to continually improve your habits by making **small changes** in direct response to real events in your life.

Over time these changes add up to amazing differences in your weight and powerful changes in your life.

You make continual improvements through a process of **daily check-ins**. A check-in is a **meeting with yourself** to plan how you can control your weight a little better. It's a time for you to **pay attention** to what's happening in your life.

The idea is to make a quick check every morning to see if you are on track. If you're off track, adjust your habits to bring yourself back on track.

What does *on track* mean? In general, you are on track if you are meeting your goals. Usually, you'll be checking that you aren't gaining weight.

Gaining weight is very easy if you don't take the time to check how you're doing. What use is it to notice that you have gained weight over the past couple of months? That's too late.

A Brown Medical School study has convincingly shown that the **quicker you notice** and respond to small weight gains, the more likely you are to maintain your weight loss.

That makes sense, doesn't it? It's harder to lose a lot of weight than it is to lose a little. If you notice a small weight gain, you can take immediate action to lose it. Tackling weight gain before it becomes a big problem is a better way to control your weight.

You don't usually have to make large adjustments. Maybe you exercise a little more, tighten up on your portion sizes, add a new habit, or reverse an unhelpful one. The idea is to notice problems quickly and **do something** before your weight spirals out of control.

What do you do in your daily check-in?

Set and Check Goals Every Day

Every day, ask yourself:

1. **Did I meet my goals?** A goal is anything you wish to accomplish. It could be a habit you want to implement, losing one pound a week or walking 2,000 extra steps a day. Goals come from your habits or your desires.
2. **What is standing in the way of meeting my goals?** Ask yourself, as honestly as you can, why didn't you meet your goals? Is there anything you can do to remove the roadblocks preventing you from meeting your goals?
3. **What are my new goals?** Make a goal of anything you think will help control your weight. It could be a weight loss goal, increasing your bench press, trying a new walking trail, checking portion sizes more carefully, or buying a set of smaller plates.
4. **How will I meet my goals?** This is where you pick habits from your Habits to Try list. It's by adopting habits that you meet your goals.

The result of asking and answering these four questions is a plan for what you want to do and a reasonable idea of how you will get there.

Why are we talking about goals? Isn't this a book on habits? The daily check-in turns goals into habits.

Remember from the introduction, a goal is a result you want to achieve, and a habit is a way of achieving a goal. You select habits from your Habits to Try list as a way of achieving your goals.

Scenario: One Pound a Week Weight Loss Goal

The most common goal is losing weight. Let's say your goal is to lose one pound a week. A very reasonable goal.

This book is full of potential habits for losing weight. Hopefully, you'll like some enough to put them on your Habits to Try list.

Let's say since it's a weekly goal, you weigh yourself every week on Sunday, and you've found you've met your one-pound weight loss goal.

Great! There's nothing to do. Keep up the good work.

Unfortunately, next Sunday, you weigh yourself, and you haven't lost one pound.

It's time to pick a weight loss-related habit from your list and try it. See if it works for you. If it works, great! If it doesn't, so what? At least you tried. Move on to another habit; maybe that one will work better.

Let's say you want to try the *Take the Stairs* habit as a way of burning a few extra calories with the hope it will be enough to get you back on track.

Goals

Habits

Habits generate new goals as part of the process. Your goal is to try to take the stairs more. Go through the four questions as a means of figuring out how you will make it actually happen.

If your work has stairs, maybe your goal will be to take the stairs twice a day at work. As part of the daily check-in, track that goal by asking yourself if you are actually using the stairs twice a day as intended.

If your habits aren't working, make changes to improve them. Experiment. Create a different habit. Try different goals. Make a little change. Imagine in your mind how it might be made to work for you.

How do you notice a little weight creep?

It would be better if you noticed any weight gain as soon as possible so you could react more quickly.

Here are several methods for noticing weight gain that you can use during your daily check-in:

- **Weigh yourself.** Weight can change so much that weighing every day can be depressing for many people. Weighing weekly may be less traumatic. If weighing yourself daily doesn't bother you, you can make a daily weigh-in part of your check-in.
- **Count calories**. Log everything you eat and count calories. A lot of apps offer calorie-counting capabilities. Even with an app, it takes a lot of discipline, but it's effective because it keeps you honest about what you eat every day.
- **Check the fit of your clothes.** When your clothes start to get tight, it's a good clue you are gaining weight.
- **Look at yourself in the mirror.** This feedback strategy works best if you're naked. You can usually tell if you are gaining weight by looking at yourself. It's easy to do before taking a shower.
- **Try on a belt.** If you usually wear loose-fitting clothes, you can try on a belt every morning when you get up. You know you are gaining weight if the belt doesn't fit well. One study found people who tied a

cord around their waist successfully kept their weight off because the cord would become tighter as they gained weight, alerting them so they could make changes.
- **Other people's opinions.** It's unlikely, but is there someone you trust to give you feedback on your weight? Just don't hold it against them if they tell you the truth!

How long does a check-in take?

A check-in doesn't have to take long. If it's going well, it may take no time at all. On other days, especially if you notice significant changes, you may need to spend more time reviewing the four questions.

When do you check-in?

Like any other habit, you are more likely to do it regularly when you pair it with some activity you already like doing.

A good time might be when you are weighing yourself in the morning or having your morning cup of coffee or a spot of tea. Find a regular time that works for you.

Another option is to schedule a meeting with yourself in your calendar. Pick a convenient time to run your daily check-in. I know you're really busy, but you're worth it, don't you think? Take the time for yourself. Your future self will thank you.

THERE ARE AS MANY WAYS TO CONTROL WEIGHT AS THERE ARE PEOPLE.

A lot of people think they know the secret to weight loss. And they aren't shy about telling you what you're doing wrong.

Some say it's one particular diet or another. Some think the only way to control your weight is to get your life under control and heal your soul. Others believe it's all about developing a better relationship with food. A hard-core group knows it's just about willpower, discipline, and calories in and calories out. An even harder-core group is sure a strict exercise routine is all you need.

In reality, it could be any of those, none of those, or something you haven't thought of yet.

You need to discover what works for you. There are a lot of habits in this book. Do I expect you to adopt every one of them? Absolutely not.

Every habit you create or discover can be used in a daily check-in. That's the real power of the daily check-in. This consistent focus on goals and habits is how you control your weight. You look at your life and learn from experience. Each day you adapt to changes in your circumstances. Each day better fits your habits to your nature and your goals. And that's what gives you the best chance at controlling your weight for the rest of your life.

3. Habit: Forgive Yourself

Forgive yourself for slip-ups as you would a friend. Don't let a lapse turn into a collapse.

This is the most important habit to adopt and the one you should try to adopt first. Why? Nobody is perfect.

Controlling your weight is a daily struggle. It's a struggle you will sometimes lose. It's a courageous task for people in our modern, obesogenic environment to control their weight.

You will slip up. It's human nature to make mistakes. It's an inevitable part of life. What matters is how you handle them.

How should you handle mistakes?

- Forgive yourself.
- Learn from them.

Forgive Yourself as You Would Forgive a Friend

What should you do about a mistake? **Forgive yourself**. Don't shame yourself. Don't let a mistake throw you off your habits. <u>Don't let a lapse become a collapse</u>.

We are often hardest on ourselves. We show ourselves less love and understanding than we would our worst enemy. You may give up if you can't see it in your heart to forgive yourself.

Forgiving yourself is called self-compassion. Self-compassion is the ability to treat yourself with kindness when things go badly. It's the secret of why some people successfully roll with life's punches, face failure with grace, and eventually overcome their problems.

Without self-compassion, you end up dwelling on failures, making your problems bigger than they really are and criticizing yourself into a downward spiral of self-loathing.

Life is tough enough without fueling the fire of your own anger and depression.

Self-compassion has three parts: self-kindness, common humanity, and mindful acceptance.

Self-kindness is being kind and understanding toward yourself rather than taking the easy road of self-criticism.

Common humanity is seeing your negative experiences as a normal part of life. Stuff happens, and it sometimes happens to you. You can deal with it. Humans are resilient.

Mindful acceptance is letting things go rather than dwelling on them.

Your emotions won't burn out of control when you practice self-compassion. You'll react more appropriately to events in your life. You'll be able to accept responsibility for your actions without feeling horrible. And your image of yourself will become less about the bad things in your life.

All these changes help you control your weight because your weight is much more likely to spin out of control when you are out of control.

Weight Gain is Information About What Doesn't Work; It's Not Failure

Once you can forgive yourself for a slip-up, it's time to reframe that negative into a positive. This is called a **growth mindset**.

A growth mindset is believing you can improve yourself through dedication, hard work, and developing good habits. A fixed mindset is the opposite; it's believing you are what you are and can't change.

Since you are reading a book about habits, you are probably a growth mindset person. You believe you can learn and develop new habits to help improve your life.

This is why a slip-up shouldn't get you down. Gaining weight is not the end of the world. It doesn't mean you should give up. It doesn't mean you are a bad person. It doesn't mean you are a failure. It means you have **learned something.**

Gaining weight is a learning opportunity. Weight gain is simply information telling you that something you are doing isn't working or your situation has changed. Your job is to try and figure out what isn't working and fix it by adjusting your habits.

Use what you've learned to do better. Think of every problem as a learning opportunity, not just evidence of how screwed up you are. If all you do is get down on yourself, you miss a chance to improve your life. Use your problems as inspiration for improvement, so you can help yourself avoid the same problems in the future.

All that matters is that you are continually learning and getting better. Time will take care of the rest.

4. Habit: Use Your Logical Brain Now

> **Use your willpower when it's the strongest to create habits that will always work, even when your willpower runs out.**

Like many people, I contribute to my savings account by having money automatically deducted from my paycheck. I wouldn't save nearly as much money if the process weren't automatic.

Think what I would have to do if money wasn't deducted automatically. I would get my paycheck, and then rather than spend it, I would have to write another check and deposit it into my savings account. I would have to remember to transfer funds from my checking to my savings account and then actually do it!

How often would I forget? How often would if find some other way to spend the money rather than saving? Too often.

Why? Short-term emotional thinking can overpower long-term logical thinking.

Under the influence of short-term thinking I'd rather buy a shiny new toy rather than follow the wisdom of long term thinking and save my money instead.

How do I get around this problem? My logical mind knows I need to save for retirement. So when I am at my most rational, that is, when I don't have cash in my hot little hands ready to spend, I set up an automatic deduction. That way I have no choice but to save money. It just works.

The rewards are reaped every month with no effort once the automatic deduction is set up. That's how the logical mind overcomes the emotional mind.

Plan and create your habits when you are at your most logical so that you will naturally and easily attain your goals.

Your logical mind knows you need help to control your weight. Creating habits *is* that help.

Setting up habits is like setting up an automatic deduction from your paycheck.

If you have to rely on constant motivation not to eat, always exercise, and always do the right thing, then you probably won't succeed. Few people can make that many right decisions under the continual bullying of their emotional brain.

By setting up habits when you are using your long-term logical thinking, you are giving yourself the best chance to succeed when temptation comes knocking, and you want to open the door. By creating habits, you guarantee success over the long run.

I have fond memories of applying this habit to what I have come to call my *Purge the Urge* day. One of the habits is to keep tempting foods out of your house so you won't eat them when hunger drives you to forage around your home looking for food to eat. This is "purging the urge." For me, ice cream is the temptress.

I did the deed from a position of strength. I had just eaten, so I wasn't hungry. I was thinking about creating a habit, so I was committed to throwing away the ice cream even though I had already paid for it, and I knew I would really want to eat it later.

Tossing a perfectly good gallon of ice cream into the trash was really hard! But it paid off. Later that night, when I was looking for a snack and would have usually made a big bowl of ice cream, the ice cream wasn't there, so I didn't eat it. Success!

You might be asking why I didn't keep the ice cream and eat small servings? Excellent question. That doesn't work for me with ice cream. I know I can't control myself around ice cream, so I have to **be extreme** and keep it out of the house entirely.

From time to time, I've thought I was over my ice cream problem. As a test I'd buy some, thinking I'd control myself. But I don't. I eat way too much of it. So I go extreme on this habit and don't have ice cream around. I wish I could handle it differently, but I can't. It's not worth the risk. That's my logical brain talking.

5. Habit: Out of Sight, Out of Mind

Create habits by looking at your life and determining where you can slip up. Figure out a way to remove whatever is tempting from your direct attention.

Out of Sight, Out of Mind is by far the most effective habit. You may notice how this idea cuts across so many different habits.

This habit makes use of two powerful ideas:

- The more challenging something is to do, the less likely you will do it.
- If something is out of sight, then you can't pay attention to it.

The first idea is pretty self-explanatory. Moving a goody to an out-of-the-way location, say in the very back of the topmost cabinet, means you are much more likely to stay on your couch when the goody urge hits. It's too much effort.

The second idea is a little more interesting. Moving food out of sight means you won't pay attention to it, which means you are less likely to eat it.

A big part of creating a system of habits is being creative about focusing your attention. You want to **focus your attention** on what is important and away from what's unimportant.

You may say to yourself, "I am stronger than that. I can be around anything and not be tempted." And that is surprisingly true. But little slip-ups add up.

You don't have to slip up often to make a big difference in your weight. If you have a bag of candy bars in your house and only have one extra candy bar a week, that's about four extra pounds a year just by that one simple slip-up.

Look around your life, determine what threatens your goals, and figure out how to remove them.

Get it out of your sight. Get it out of your mind. Create a world in which you do the right thing naturally.

6. Habit: Be Less Inactive

> Make a goal to be less inactive. The rest will take care of itself.

Be Less Inactive is the second most effective habit. The idea is simple: being less sedentary burns calories. It seems obvious, doesn't it?

So why not say exercise more instead? It doesn't work as well as saying be less inactive.

If you say exercise more, people feel you are ordering them around, so they naturally resist. People like to have a choice.

Once you give people a choice of how not to be inactive, they will naturally find other things to do, and many will be physical activity.

The research of Dr. Leonard Epstein, Professor of Pediatrics and Psychology at the University of Buffalo, has found that kids who reduced their inactive behavior lost weight, improved fitness, and maintained their weight loss.

In his research, **they did not tell the kids what to do.** They didn't say to play basketball or go for a run. Instead, **they encouraged kids not to be idle** and let them figure out what to do for themselves.

A lot of what the kids did instead was be physically active, resulting in better health. When kids were told to exercise, the results weren't as good. Kids like choice. So do adults.

One habit is restricting the amount of TV and other media (games, music, etc.) you consume to no more than a couple of hours a day. This lets you decide how to spend the rest of your time. The odds are you will naturally spend more time being active.

Do you see how this works? You aren't telling yourself to exercise. You just aren't letting yourself be inactive by watching TV. You'll naturally be more active when you no longer have the option of being inactive. It's a twisted yet fantastic idea.

Other activities need to be available for this habit to work. It won't work if there's nothing else to do. You'll need to be creative.

7. Habit: Adopt an Exercise Mindset

If you believe you are exercising, your body will respond as if it is exercising.

The *Hotel Maids* study is one of the most bizarre studies of all time. It found that if you think of physical activity as exercise, your body will respond as if it is exercise. When you expect to see results, you are more likely to see results.

Isn't all physical activity exercise? Not if you don't think it is.

Hotel housekeepers do a lot of physical labor. Cleaning hotel rooms is hard work. This study found that housekeepers often didn't think of their job as exercise. When asked if they exercise regularly, many didn't think they did. They actually exercised a lot; they just didn't think of it as exercise.

What's odd is their body didn't seem to treat their work as exercise.

The study divided the housekeepers into two groups; for the *control* group, nothing changed. They went about their job as usual.

The second group was the *informed* group. They were asked to change their mindset, to think of their job as exercise, not merely physical activity.

The results were dramatic. The informed women lost 2 pounds in just four weeks. They also lowered their blood pressure, BMI, and body-fat percentage. That's a significant change in only four weeks.

As interesting as this is, why does it matter to you?

Many of the habits in this book are about finding little extra bits of physical activity. This study shows how you think about that extra activity is important.

Change your mindset. When you find extra bits of physical activity, like climbing the stairs, think of it as exercise. You'll see better results.

8. Habit: Make Things Fun and Easy

Pick the fun way, the easy way, not the most effective way.

Here's some good news: your logical mind may guilt you into doing the most effective and efficient thing, but that's not the best way to build a long-term habit.

How should you create a habit so you can do it for the rest of your life? Make it **fun and easy**.

Isn't that good news? Harder isn't better. Torturing yourself isn't better. Optimal isn't better. What's better is picking habits you can do and want to do.

Actively seek out ways to make your habits fun and easy. You have permission from both research and common sense. Not only will you get better results, but your life will also improve.

Habits aren't a punishment. The funner something is to do, and the easier it is to do, the more likely you will keep doing it. And isn't that what a habit is?

Achieving a goal is important, but so is how you get there. If you don't enjoy something, you will likely quit before the habit can kick in.

Here's a great example of making something fun. In Sweden, they wanted to encourage more people to take the stairs, so they made the stairs play music when you walked up them. Adding that little bit of fun encouraged 66% more people to take the stairs rather than ride the escalator.

Pick the most fun workout you can do at the gym, not the most effective. I know that's not what all the fitness influencers say, but who cares? Unless you are a professional athlete, doing something is far more important than doing something perfectly, especially if the alternative is doing nothing at all.

Combine a workout with something you enjoy doing. I read a book while I'm on my elliptical machine. Let me tell you; it's much easier to last an hour on the elliptical when I want to keep reading my book! Other people listen to podcasts or watch videos. Find something that will keep you motivated.

Pick the funnest diet that's easy to implement, not the most restrictive—if possible.

Walk or bike along a scenic route.

Make it a game.

Track your progress in an app.

Exercise with a group.

Try something really different, like exercising in VR.

You get the idea; it's obvious once you think about it, but it's easy to underestimate how important this habit is.

Be creative. Be thoughtful. Be persistent. Really try to internalize the idea that making something fun and easy dramatically increases your chances of keeping habits over the long run.

9. Habit: Bring Your Goal Picture to Mind

> **Power through adversity by thinking of a mental picture of how you wish to look, feel, eat, act and think.**

Your *goal picture* is **your identity**. It's a mental picture of how you wish to look, feel, eat, act and think. It is a **complete picture of who you want to be as a person.**

It may contain many overlapping images, feelings, and thoughts. It may be a series of pictures, like a movie. It may be an ideal, like *I am a person who exercises*, or *I am a person who eats a healthy diet*, or *I am a person who never gives up*.

There will be times when you feel weak and unmotivated. You will want to quit. At these times, bring your goal picture to mind; it will help you remember who you are trying to be. Sometimes that's all you need to outlast temptation.

The goal picture also works at the subconscious level to change the subconscious image you have of yourself. We often resist change because we see ourselves only a certain way. Our old image locks us into position. Your goal picture allows you to become the person you want to be.

Steps to Creating Your Goal Picture

Here are the steps to building your goal picture:

- Think about who and what you want to be.
- Be honest with your goals. Don't set yourself up for failure.
- Think about how you wish to look, feel, eat, act and think.
- If you have difficulty creating a picture, think about people you admire and what you like about them.
- Picture your existing body, then picture the new body you want.
- Picture exactly how you wish to look down to the smallest detail.
- Picture exactly how you wish to feel.
- Picture what you wish to eat and in what quantities.

- Picture exactly how you wish to act in specific situations.
- Picture exactly how you wish to think in specific situations.
- Make the changes real in your imagination. Begin to experience yourself as you want to be. Experience the changes you have made.
- Make as many pictures as you need.

Keep building your goal picture in your mind until you can quickly call it up without too much effort.

You don't have to follow every step. Some of the steps may not make sense to you. Feel free to include only what you think will motivate you when you need to be motivated.

Pack your goal picture with vibrant symbols overflowing with personal meaning. When you look at or think about your goal picture, you want its meaning to be instantly clear. Don't worry about what other people will think.

If your motivation to exercise is best symbolized by an old pair of track shoes you wore in high school, then pick that as your symbol for exercise.

All the motivation and health you felt at that time will be accessible via the track shoe symbol. Picking a different, more conventional symbol would drain it of all its power. That's the idea for all your goal picture symbols: make them deeply meaningful to you.

My goal picture is simple because I am not a very good visualizer:

I picture Superman looking up at a blazing sun and a full moon set against a green background. Green means good health to me because it symbolizes the vibrancy of nature. Superman symbolizes strength and goodness. The sun symbolizes vast power and endless energy. The moon symbolizes the loved ones and relationships I'll lose if I don't succeed. And the long distance between Superman and the sun reminds me of how far I have to go and that I want to live a long time. When I need more strength, I transform the sun into a roaring bear standing tall on its hind legs, claws extended. I imagine myself infused with the same power and energy a bear must feel in full roar.

In my mind, these are the images that motivate me. They may seem laughably silly to you, but that's OK. You need to come up with images that are personally meaningful to you. It doesn't matter what they are.

Let your goal picture change as your life changes. It is never complete. Change it as you find new issues that need handling.

How to Apply Your Goal Picture

Bring your goal picture to mind whenever you feel like you need support and motivation. This could be when you are overeating or when you want to quit exercising, or for any other reason.

Mentally visit each symbol in the picture. Think about what each symbol means to you. Let your thoughts and feelings fill you with renewed strength and purpose.

Sometimes your spirit just runs out of gumption, and you need a refill. That's what your goal picture does for you. Visualizing your goal picture pumps you up when you need help the most.

The great thing about this process is your habits and identity reinforce each other. Your identity helps you follow your habits, and your habits help create your identity. It's a win-win.

10. Habit: Lifeguarding

> Save yourself from slip-ups by becoming your own lifeguard.

Your brain is amazing, but that doesn't mean it is optimal or perfect in design. It can have flaws, **like feeling unwanted urges to eat.** Thoughts of eating show up in your mind, and chances are you will eat because your brain is telling you, "I'm hungry."

See a luscious ad for dessert, and suddenly your brain inserts thoughts of hunger when you weren't hungry a second ago.

The smell in freshly baked bread as you walk by a bakery will immediately turn your thoughts to eating, when a moment before, you may have been thinking about the warmth of the sun on your face.

Or perhaps your internal hunger control mechanisms are broken, and you become hungry long before you should.

Whatever the reason, unwanted urges to eat can haunt you. You don't want them, yet they appear in your mind anyway. Because these are your thoughts, you think they are real, so you should act on them.

And that's the problem: **you eat unnecessarily because of unwanted thoughts.**

If you understand that these thoughts are often just brain noise, like static on TV, you can avoid eating just because you have thoughts of eating.

Not only thoughts about eating can be unwanted. In the middle of exercising, have you ever thought something like: you've done enough now, you are tired, and it's time to stop now?

Where does that thought come from? In most cases, it's not true; there's no reason to stop, but if you think your "stop exercising" thoughts are real, you'll probably stop.

Yet in most cases, your urge to stop exercising is no more real than your urge to eat.

In general, overcoming unwanted thoughts will help you do two things:

- **Stop doing** something you don't think you should be doing—like overeating.
- **Keep doing** something you think you should be doing—like exercising.

A lot of unwanted thoughts may flow through your mind. To control your weight, we'll be concerned mainly with the urges compelling you to eat and the ones demanding you stop exercising—in other words, thoughts that lead to slip-ups.

Not All Your Thoughts Deserve Your Attention

At any time, a variety of thoughts fly through your mind, possibly like:

> Eat the cookies...it doesn't matter anymore...I can have all the ice cream I want...nobody cares...if I have another candy bar, I'll feel better...I am a giant fat pig anyway...I am such a loser.

You may have had thoughts like these all your life.

There is a **big secret** about your thoughts you may not know: **just because you have a thought doesn't mean you have to pay attention to it.**

Many thoughts are just unwanted messages from your brain that you can safely ignore. I call these **pop-thoughts** because they pop into your mind and will just as quickly disappear if you let them.

Cognitive scientists estimate that over 95% of your thinking is below the conscious level. That means less than 5% of your thoughts are made consciously and most of your thoughts happen automatically.

A typical example is what happens when driving a car on a long trip. When it's over, drivers often don't remember driving at all, yet they somehow complete a long, complicated journey. Clearly, driving requires a lot of thinking, but you are not always aware of it.

If you can drive without thinking, you can certainly eat without thinking!

You are Not Your Thoughts

What this all means is **your thoughts are not you.** Thoughts pop into your head for many reasons, and not all of those reasons make sense.

Typically we think **all** of our thoughts are important because, well, we think our thoughts are us.

Please consider that the voice in your head may sometimes be speaking rubbish that you can simply ignore. This is a pretty **radical idea**. We are not used to thinking that some of our thoughts may be unimportant; or even more radical, that many of our thoughts may be harmful.

Let's say you have a thought that you are hungry. Why did you get this thought? Where did it come from? Why did it show up just now? Why didn't you have this thought a little earlier or later?

Even after finishing a big meal, you can still think about eating more. You know you can't be hungry. You just ate a giant meal!

Where did this thought come from? Consider that it might just be an unwanted message from your brain. The key is to recognize this thought as unwanted so you don't react to it. Imagine what would happen if you ate whenever you thought you were hungry? Unfortunately, most of us don't have to imagine.

Here's a quote from the actor Willem Defoe about what his brain tells him:

> **Ever since puberty, whenever I cross a bridge, I've felt a compulsion to jump off. I feel the same impulse with balconies. —Willem Dafoe**

Do you think he should pay attention to this message from his brain?

You don't need a death wish to get the same thought as Mr. Defoe. These kinds of thoughts may pop into your head.

Where do they come from? Why do you get them? Nobody really knows.

It's easy to say to ignore these thoughts, but they often grab your attention with such strength and persistence that they are hard to let go of.

In Mr. Dafoe's case, he has ignored these thoughts because he doesn't want to die a painful death. In the same way, many other messages from your brain should be dismissed because they aren't any more real. They are just pop thoughts.

Have you ever had thoughts like *you are stupid, you are ugly, you'll never amount to anything?* Where do these horrible little thoughts come from? In your better moments, you know they aren't true, but they can still hurt—a lot.

They are just **unwanted messages from your brain,** and you don't have to pay attention to them. Let these thoughts pass through you. They are just mental events. They don't reflect reality. They come, and they go. They only have a life if you give them attention. It's your mental attention that strengthens unwanted thoughts. Ignore them, and they will go away.

The idea that you can consciously choose which thoughts to pay attention to is a radical and powerful idea, one of the most potent ideas you may ever hear.

Just What are You Thinking? Keep a Thought Log

Do this exercise. As you go about your day, write down all your thoughts for a half hour. Be sure to write down all your thoughts. Don't only write down your big thoughts like *I have to go grocery shopping*. Write down all the quick automatic thoughts you may have but do not always realize you are having because they seem so natural. When you see someone walking toward you, for example, you may immediately think *What an ugly shirt*. Write down all of those kinds of thoughts too.

Afterward, take a look at all the thoughts you have written down. What do you think of your thoughts? Some are probably untrue, trivial, mean, or bizarre. Some may be wise, kind, and insightful. And other thoughts may not seem like you at all. You may be surprised to find your thoughts are all over the map.

After looking at your thoughts: Do you think all your thoughts are equally valid or equally important? Do you think all your thoughts should be given equal weight?

Some Thoughts are Unwanted

It's likely you don't want some of your thoughts. You probably don't want, for example, that thought of eating an extra piece of cake when you've already had a piece.

When is a thought unwanted?

- **When it doesn't make sense to you.** It's a thought telling you to eat when you aren't hungry, a thought to stop exercising when you should keep on going, or a thought telling yourself to jump off a cliff when the jump would kill you!
- **When it doesn't conform to who you want to be.** You have an image of the person you want to be. That's your identity. You know how you want to act. Any thought that doesn't agree with the person you want to be can be considered an unwanted message from your brain.

How can you deal with unwanted thoughts and urges? Through a process, I call **Lifeguarding.** A lifeguard saves lives by the same process you can use to manage unwanted thoughts. Once you can manage your unwanted thoughts, you can manage slip-ups.

Think about how lifeguards perform their job:

- **Go on guard.** When lifeguards go on duty, they immediately become sensitive to everything around them. Anyone could need their help at any time. In the same way, you can go on guard when you enter a potential slip-up situation. You need to go on guard when you are near food or exercising. At any time, you could need your help to stop eating or to keep exercising. Once you are on guard, it's time to be on the lookout for trouble.

- **Scan for signs.** Lifeguards continually scan the environment looking for potential problems to enable a reaction before a situation becomes an emergency. In the same way, you can scan your thoughts, visual images, feelings, and surroundings for signs of trouble. When you find something wrong, it's time to fix the problem.
- **Respond skillfully.** When lifeguards detect a problem, the job is not done. Lifeguards must skillfully respond to any situation, or lives will be lost. In the same way, when you detect a slip-up situation, you must react skillfully to save yourself from the slip-up.

You don't have to be a victim of your random thoughts. Realize that thoughts happen to you despite your intentions, not because of them. You can learn to retrain your brain to stop unwanted thoughts, and we'll use Lifeguarding as part of the retraining.

Retraining Your Brain to Stop Unwanted Thoughts

You can retrain your brain to stop sending you unwanted messages because of something called **neuroplasticity.**

Neuroplasticity is the ability of the brain to change itself. Once thought impossible, we now know, as Michael Merzenich tells us in Scientific American, "The brain was constructed to change." And from Dr. Jeffrey Schwartz's groundbreaking book *The Mind and The Brain,* we learn, "The willful directing of attention can act on the brain to alter its subsequent patterns of activity."

This means that your brain is not hard-wired into its current behavior. Your brain can be retrained to reverse the years of bad weight-gaining habits.

One way to look at some of your current thinking processes is that they are like an old two-lane highway that needs to be replaced by a new high-speed freeway. For years, when you've needed to go from A to B, you've only been able to go on the old highway. There's only been one road, and you've never had a choice to go any other way. You just got on the road and went. You knew the road so well that you didn't have to think during the trip.

Rethink Yourself a New Brain

You can rethink yourself a new brain. The key is changing your behavior.

Changing your behavior changes your brain. Why? Because it quiets activity in one part of your brain and shifts it to a new part. If you can consistently shift your attention away from the thoughts and behaviors you don't want, you can change the physical structure of your brain. You are building a new highway and tearing down the old.

Focusing your attention on a replacement behavior causes new synapses to fire, strengthening those connections in your brain. After a while, the old connections in your brain associated with the old thoughts and behaviors will weaken. You'll increasingly turn to a new way of thinking and behaving because those pathways in your brain are stronger.

You might think this is all just mumbo jumbo. But it isn't. Dr. Schwartz has convincingly documented this fantastic capability of your brain. Your brain can change and how you direct your attention is the force that makes the change.

The **choices you make now matter** because they will influence the choices you'll make in the future. If you are willing to put in the work, you can literally retrain your brain away from old habits you no longer want into new habits that better represent who you want to become.

The Three Steps to Retraining Your Brain

You can retrain your brain away from old behaviors using a series of steps I adapted from Dr. Jeffrey Schwartz's book, *Brain Lock*. The steps to retraining your brain are as follows:

1. **Become aware of your thoughts.** When you notice an unwanted thought, go to step 2.
2. **Tell Yourself: It's Not Me; It's Just an Unwanted Message from My Brain!** Saying this statement to yourself identifies the thought as an unwanted

thought you shouldn't take seriously or pay attention to.

3. **Immediately switch behaviors.** Changing your behavior changes how your brain is wired.

These steps aim to focus your mind on solutions rather than problems. If you can shift your attention from problems to solutions frequently enough, your brain will reconnect itself to support your new solution-solving behaviors.

STEP 1: BECOME AWARE OF YOUR OWN THOUGHTS

The first step in the retraining process is becoming aware of your thoughts. This combines the *go on guard* and *scan for signs* Lifeguarding steps. Once you are aware of your thoughts, you can decide which thoughts are unwanted and which thoughts you should pay attention to.

You can become aware of your thoughts through a process called **mental note-taking.** Mental note-taking is similar to what you did when you wrote down your thought log. When a thought happens, you name or label it. Your goal is to observe your thoughts as they arise.

For mental note-taking to work, you must stand outside yourself as an observer. You need to be able to observe your thoughts as they happen. This skill, also called "mindful awareness" or "bare attention," is described as calmly viewing your experience as an outsider.

Mental note-taking is so different and strange from everyday thinking that you may find it challenging to do. That's OK. It's a skill you get better at with practice. You usually think and act without much thinking about what you are thinking. You are being asked to do something different. Be patient. The payoff is worth it.

Mental Note Taking Example: Walking

We'll use walking as our first example of mental note-taking. Walking is a fun example because it's so simple and automatic that we don't realize how complicated it is.

Also, it's slightly easier to take mental notes of a physical activity like walking than it is of pure thinking. We'll move on to mental note-taking for thoughts in our following example.

Let's say you are sitting down and need to stand up to walk. What might your mental notes look like? In our examples, mental notes are marked with the phrase "note as."

Getting up from sitting requires a decision, which can be noted. On the decision to walk, note it as *wanting to walk*. The note is a thought about your thought. You generate the note by watching your thoughts as they happen.

When rising from your sitting position, note it as *rising*. When standing, note as *standing*. When looking from here to your intended destination, note as *looking, seeing*.

At first, when you are walking, note as *right step, left step*. After practicing right and left steps for a while, you can break down each step into smaller components. For each step, try noting it as *raising, dropping*. After you practice that for a while, you can become even more detailed. For each step, note it as *raising, pushing forward, or dropping*.

After you have walked enough and you decide to sit down again, note as *wanting to sit down*.

That's it. You're done with the example. Keep trying this exercise until it feels natural. You will probably feel completely awkward and a bit silly when you try it for the first time. You may not even be able to note simple actions like *right step*. There won't be enough time. The step will happen, you won't have noted it, and you won't believe how you couldn't note such a simple thing.

After you try it for a while, you'll notice that you can make mental comments about many of your actions without tripping. Then you'll notice you can make mental comments about most of your actions. And eventually, you'll be able to notice more and more of your actions with ever finer levels of detail.

The point of this exercise is to learn **to comment on what you are doing and thinking mentally.** Once you can do that, it gives you space to see if a thought is unwanted. And once you know a thought is unwanted, you can deal with it by moving immediately to the next step.

Step 2: Tell Yourself: It's Not Me; It's Just an Unwanted Message from My Brain!

Using *mental note-taking,* as you have a thought think about it and see if it is unwanted. If the thought doesn't make sense or doesn't conform to who you want to be, then say to yourself:

It's Not Me; It's Just an Unwanted Message from My Brain!

When you notice an unwanted message from your brain, saying this statement to yourself identifies the thought for what it really is and interrupts your thought process so you can move to the *Immediately Switch Behaviors* step. In the beginning, it can help to say the phrase out loud. This is part of the *respond skillfully* Lifeguarding step.

Each phrase in *It's Not Me; It's Just an Unwanted Message from My Brain!* has a purpose.

The *It's Not Me* part is to remind yourself that you can't help which thoughts pop into your mind. You are not your thoughts. You don't consciously control your thoughts. Blaming yourself for your thoughts would be like blaming yourself for an itch you feel on your arm. You wouldn't think of blaming yourself for an itch. Don't blame yourself for your thoughts, either.

The *It's Just an Unwanted Message from My Brain!* part is to remind yourself that this is a pop thought. It's simply a thought that popped into your mind. Thoughts are not under your control, so don't worry about them.

Expect that you will have these thoughts. You will have these thoughts every day of your life. Understanding that will help you recognize and respond to them sooner.

And that's what is essential to keep in mind. You are learning to be aware of your thoughts and then consciously deciding how to respond to them. If you decide that a thought is unwanted, then apply the next step: *Immediately Switch Behaviors.*

Step 3: Immediately Switch Behaviors

After becoming aware of an unwanted thought and having said it to yourself

It's Not Me; It's Just an Unwanted Message from My Brain!, immediately **replace** your current behavior with a better activity.

The replacement activity can be **anything you enjoy doing.** Your goal is to focus your attention on your new activity. Ideally, your replacement behavior should be **active, helpful, constructive,** and **require concentration** and **strategy.**

Involving other people is a good idea. Biking alone, for example, is not as effective as biking with another person because it is less likely to refocus your attention on the new replacement activity. And passive activities don't work very well. You need to be active, or your attention may drift back to your unwanted thoughts.

There are two different types of replacement activities: **Active Replacement** and **Drop the Thought.**

Active Replacement

Your goal is to immediately do something to interrupt the unwanted thought and replace it with an alternate, more desirable activity.

Some possible replacement activities are:

- Go for a walk or a bike ride.
- Work in your garden.
- Yoga.
- Play with your kids or your dog.
- Meditate.
- Talk to a friend.
- Play team basketball.
- Breathe deeply if you are in an awkward situation where you can't free yourself.

Can you think of other replacement activities based on your life and interests?

Switch for 15 Minutes

Have a goal of engaging in your replacement behavior for a minimum of 15 minutes. Dr. Schwartz found this to be about the time needed for urges to be noticeably reduced.

Drop the Thought

Ignoring an unwanted thought may be your only option when you are in a situation where you can't respond actively. Thought-dropping is not as effective as an active response, but sometimes it's the best you can do, and it's a lot better than obsessing over an unwanted thought.

To drop a thought, just breathe, relax into your body, and let the unwanted thought drift through and out of your mind. A thought stays alive when you keep thinking about it. Do not think about it at all. Just let the thought pass through you like a gentle breeze. You may be tempted to analyze the thought, dissect it, and figure out where it came from and what you should do about it. Don't. It's an unwanted message. You don't owe it anything. Don't let it own you. Ignore it.

Slowly Changing Your Brain

Over time the three-step brain retraining process retrains your brain away from unwanted thoughts and activities. Your brain actually changes to a new set of behaviors.

It's not enough to tell yourself not to eat. That's why self-talk isn't as effective a strategy. You already know you shouldn't do something, yet you will still feel compelled to do it anyway. Unless you switch to another behavior, you won't be making the physical changes in your brain that will help prevent unwanted thoughts in the future.

Lifeguarding Example: Strolling the Food Court

Let's run through an example of Lifeguarding while walking into a food court at your local mall.

As you walk in, you know you are entering a danger zone where slip-ups are likely.

Entering a danger zone means it's time to **go on guard** by observing your thoughts using mental note-taking. A true master is always on guard, but that's a skill developed over time. For now, it's a great start to notice when you are in a danger zone and then to go on guard.

What thoughts might go through your mind as you walk the food court?

> That cinnamon roll looks incredible. Note as seeing food.
>
> Oh, the smell is heavenly—freshly baked dough...sweet icing...thick with cinnamon. Note as smelling food.
>
> Maybe I should get one? Note as wanting to eat.
>
> Oh, I am wanting to eat because I smelled the cinnamon roll. Let's see if this is an unwanted thought. Yes, it is. I can't have a cinnamon roll right now. It would blow my calorie budget, and I would rather have a nice dinner tonight.
>
> So: It's Not Me; It's Just an Unwanted Message from My Brain!
>
> Now, what behavior will I switch to? I don't have a lot of options in the mall. I'll breathe deeply and drop the thought. I'll turn my thoughts to what I am looking for here and walk faster past the tempting sights and smells.

And that's it. Once you're out of the danger zone, you can go off guard again. It's not a complex process. What makes it possible is your ability to pay attention to your thoughts, think about what they mean, and then decide what to do based on your evaluation of the thought. For those prone to obesity, this is the **highest possible form** of weight control.

Previously you might have just smelled the cinnamon roll, bought it, eaten it, and then afterward wondered how you could have let yourself eat 1,000 calories in a single dessert. Oh, the torment of hindsight!

Lifeguarding gives you a tool to interrupt that automatic behavior cycle and return control to where it belongs—you.

Lifeguarding expands far beyond helping with automatic eating. If you have any negative thoughts about yourself, Lifeguarding can help with those too.

Lifeguarding really can apply to every part of your life. *Go on guard* can apply to any potential slip-up situation. *Scan for signs* can be any way you notice that you are entering a danger zone. And *respond skillfully* can make use of any habit in this book or any strategy you create.

Lifeguarding is potentially one of this book's most potent and life-transforming habits.

If you can master Lifeguarding, you'll have a skill nobody can take away, and you'll have it for the rest of your life.

11. Habit: Manage Your Automatic Eating Triggers

A trigger is any event, feeling, or situation in which you are tempted to eat automatically.

Have you ever opened up a bag of potato chips, ate the first chip, and then hundreds of hundreds of calories later realized you ate the whole bag? You probably don't even remember eating after the third bite. What happened?

That's automatic eating. It's eating when you don't even realize you're eating. It is eating mechanically, without thinking, one bite after another.

Who hasn't had this experience in some form or another? It doesn't have to be potato chips. It could be cookies or candy or anything.

Imagine if, day after day, most of your eating habits were on automatic pilot. You would eat automatically and without thought. You would eat more than you wanted to, things you didn't want to, and when you didn't want to. You wouldn't stop eating when you should. You would barely remember eating. And you would gain weight year after year.

Sound familiar?

That's why you need to develop habits to overcome automatic eating.

The first habit is to recognize when you are eating automatically. By identifying what triggers your automatic eating, you can put yourself in an excellent position to stop the triggers.

When Do You Eat Automatically?

The first step in recognizing your triggers is to think about the times you eat automatically. Some common automatic eating triggers are:

- **Trigger Feelings:** stressed, anxious, lonely, sad, depressed, hungry, happy, bored, tired, angry, hopeless, a lack of control in your life, unappreciated.

- **Trigger Events:** party, sport, vacation, concert, funeral.
- **Trigger Situations:** stressful, embarrassing, alone, watching TV, going to the movies, talking on the phone, doing homework, sitting at the computer, reading, visiting a relative, driving in your car.
- **Trigger Foods:** candy, chocolate, ice cream, potato chips, pasta, fries.

It's almost anywhere or anytime.

A visit from parents is an automatic eating trigger situation for some people. If it is for you, you know that you are in a trigger situation when your parents are visiting, and you need to be more vigilant.

Some people find breakfast a trigger situation. Mornings are hectic, and the brain isn't fully awake, and without thinking, they will grab a donut.

Other examples are buying a big bag of popcorn when you go to a movie, eating junk food while lying on the couch watching TV, eating candy while reading or studying, going to a party with lots of food begging to be wolfed down, worrying about an upcoming test or seeing a box of cookies on a table.

Sometimes you may not realize you have eaten automatically until after you've finished. In these situations, trace your day to determine the trigger. You can start to deal with your triggers once you know them.

What are my triggers?

How can you deal with your triggers? There are a few ways:

- **Avoid Trigger Situations.** Discretion is often the better part of valor. Sometimes the best way to avoid automatic eating situations is to run away and save yourself. Don't feel you must be macho and tackle every trigger situation head-on. It's up to you to figure out how extreme you need to be.
- **Dump Trigger Foods.** Dump all the foods you know tempt you to eat automatically. If it isn't available, you can't eat it. In a trigger situation, you're one short mindless moment away from tearing open a bag of cookies or popping the lid off a big container of ice cream. Just get rid of all these items. Ask a friend to help you dump all your trigger foods for support.
- **Make a Special Effort to Eat Joyfully.** You often feel compelled to eat in a trigger situation. In difficult situations, focus on eating your food joyfully. Sometimes reconnecting to the physical feelings in your body can kick you out of automatic eating. We'll talk about Joyful Eating in a later chapter.

These suggestions can help with many of your triggers, but not all of them. Sometimes you can't avoid a trigger situation, sometimes, trigger food surrounds you, and you can't help it, and sometimes even eating joyfully won't help. For those extra difficult situations, consider turning to the *Lifeguarding* habit.

12. Habit: Visualize Your Automatic Eating Scenarios

Visualize your automatic eating trigger situations and imagine how you would handle them.

There's an old saying: luck favors the prepared mind. You can improve your success in dealing with automatic eating by visualizing how you want to handle these situations before they even happen.

Don't Skip Visualization! It works.

When most people see a section on visualization, they skip it and move on to something seemingly more important. That might be a mistake.

Visualization trains your brain almost as well as doing the real thing without all the physical effort. And because you can visualize a scenario far more times than you can perform it, visualization is an incredibly cheap and efficient way of changing your brain. That's why world-class athletes are taught visualization as part of their training. Please give it a try.

There are three steps to visualizing your automatic eating scenarios:

- List Your Triggers
- List Your Replacement Activities
- Visualize How You'll Handle Each Scenario

Step 1: List Your Triggers

Earlier, we listed several possible eating triggers. Now it's time to create a list of your triggers so you can visualize how you will handle them.

Ask yourself: when are you likely to eat automatically? Take some time with this one. Think back to when you've done so. What have you eaten when you didn't want to? What were the situations? Where were you? Who was with you?

Why do you think you ended up eating? Please write down your answers. Hopefully, you can handle many situations by removing your trigger foods and avoiding trigger situations, as we talked about in the *Managing Your Triggers* habit, but unfortunately, not all scenarios are so easily solved.

Step 2: List Your Replacement Activities

Next, create your list of possible activities you can switch to when responding to an automatic eating trigger. We listed several in the Lifeguarding habit, but you'll also need to think of some of your own that fit your life and personality.

By creating your replacement activity list ahead of time, you won't have to think about when to switch activities. You can do it.

Keep in mind that you can **drop any unwanted thoughts.** You can ignore the thought and let it pass through you and out of your mind.

Step 3: Visualize How You'll Handle Each Scenario

Now that you've created your list of triggers and possible replacement activities, it's time to visualize each trigger situation and imagine how you would react.

Think about a trigger. Think about what you will say and do when you encounter it. Keep going through all the trigger situations you've identified until you are confident that the next time you will know what to do when they happen. When a trigger does come up, you should be in an excellent position to counter it because you will have already practiced handling it. Your brain will have already started making changes toward the new behaviors.

When you find a new trigger, run through this same process again. Find an appropriate replacement activity and visualize how you will handle it when it happens.

Here are a few triggers we'll use as examples:

- Food Advertisement Comes on While Watching TV
- Hungry in a Meeting
- Urge to Stop Halfway through an Exercise Routine
- I am Stupid or Fat or Ugly or a Failure

You will certainly be able to come up with many more of your own.

Scenario: Food Advertisement Comes on While Watching TV

Lusciously shot commercials of cookies and candy bars can immediately excite your mind with cravings that, if left unchecked, may turn directly into overeating. What can you do?

Watching less TV is always a good answer :-)

Another strategy is to watch all TV on record so you can skip the food commercials.

What else can you do if neither of those approaches will work? Go through the Lifeguarding steps.

On seeing a food advertisement, *go on guard* immediately and start *scanning for signs* of cravings and thoughts using *mental note-taking*. Then *respond skillfully* to the ad.

One possible skillful response is to skip past the commercial if you are watching from a recording. For live TV watchers, consider changing the channel so you won't be affected by the commercial.

If neither of these responses works and your thought scans reveals a buildup of unwanted binge-provoking cravings, it's time to move to step number two of *Retraining Your Brain*.

Say to yourself: *It's Not Me; It's Just an Unwanted Message from My Brain!* Then *immediately switch behaviors*.

You may leave the room (stay away from the kitchen!). Try breathing deeply and dropping the thought. Or try something else from your replacement activities list.

Using Lifeguarding, you don't have to let commercials compel you to eat. You can do something about it. You have the power.

Scenario: Hungry in a Meeting

You are in an important meeting with ten other people, and it happens: you suddenly are tempted by the plate of donuts or bagels your coworker has generously brought. Oh no! Making an active response to the thought is impossible because you must stay in the meeting.

In this situation, **start deep breathing and drop the thought**. You don't have to react to the temptation. You don't have to pay it any attention. It's just a thought. Let the thought flow through you. The more you think about it, the more energy is pumped into the thought, and the bigger it gets. You'll be forced to act on the thought when it gets big enough. Shrink the thought. Ignore it, and it will shrink to nothing and go away.

Scenario: Urge to Stop Halfway through an Exercise Routine

You are about halfway through your exercise routine, and all of a sudden, you're starting to get thoughts like these:

You've done enough already and are tired; it's time to stop now...Hey, you can stop now...Oh, you can eat that piece of leftover birthday cake; after all, you deserve it; you exercised so hard today.

I get thoughts like these all the time. What can you do about them? Lifeguarding to the rescue.

When you start exercising, *go on guard*. Almost every exercise routine will likely, at one time or another, prompt your brain to tell you to stop before you're done.

While exercising, *scan for signs* of thoughts about stopping using *mental note-taking*.

If you become aware of an impulse to stop, determine if it's an unwanted thought. Sometimes you may be hurt or drained enough that stopping is precisely what you should do. But most of the time, quitting while exercising isn't who you want to be, so it's an unwanted thought.

It's time to *respond skillfully*. What are some possible responses to thoughts demanding you stop exercising before you are ready? *Drop the thought* is one possible response, but you may prefer one of the more active responses we've discussed, something positive that will help pump you up and motivate you. It's a good opportunity to *Bring Your Goal Picture to Mind*.

You don't have to pick just one habit, but you can use them all. And I'm sure you will create strategies of your own. Lifeguarding helps you **realize when it's time to use a habit.**

A lot of the time, you might just accept the thought of quitting exercising and stop. Using Lifeguarding, you will realize when a thought is unwanted, and then you'll be able to implement your plan to deal with it.

Some people may be tempted to use a negative strategy like repeating something horrible to themselves, like "I'm so fat I have to keep exercising." Avoid this. Always keep it positive. Negative motivation never lasts long and does a lot of damage along the way.

Scenario: I am Stupid or Fat or Ugly or a Failure

This scenario lets you know that Lifeguarding helps you deal with much more than automatic eating. You can respond to these unwanted thoughts using the same techniques. You don't have to let your brain put you down. Fight back. Retrain these thoughts out of your brain so you can have a better, more positive life. You deserve it.

13. Habit: Sherlock Holmes Your Hidden Patterns

Audit how you spend your money and your time to find any unexpected patterns holding you back.

This is like automatic eating but expanded to your entire life.

Have you ever wondered: why can't I control my weight? I think I'm doing pretty well.

The cause may be **hidden patterns of behavior**.

How can your behaviors be hidden from you? When they are below your conscious awareness.

What kind of patterns? Maybe you stop every morning for a high-calorie drink...go out after work for pizza and beer...stop for donuts on the weekend...skip your daily walks...eat two candy bars instead of one...buy a cake every time you go shopping...work late more than expected...skip working out because you are tired...buy fast food instead of cooking...cut your workouts short.

And so on and so on and so on. The list of potential ways you can lose control of your weight is endless.

These everyday behaviors are the kind of things that can slip easily under your conscious awareness. You do them without thinking, yet they hugely impact weight control.

How do you find these hidden patterns? Through **money and time**.

How you spend your money and how you spend your time reveals a lot about your life. They deeply relate to each other.

Keep a Time and Expense Log

How do we turn this insight into a habit? Track what you spend your money on and how you spend your time.

For money, use a credit card to make purchases, then your expenses will be itemized on bank statements. If you don't have a credit card, combine time tracking with expense tracking.

Time is harder track. You'll have to keep a detailed log of how you spend your time. Write down everything you do (and spend). I know it's a pain, but the results are worth it.

Use Your Daily Check-in

When starting this habit, look at your bank statements for the last six months. After that's done, pick one day a week or month to regularly audit your expense and time log.

You're looking for any emerging patterns. Go over every line. Is it unexpected? Is it more than you thought? Is it less than you thought?

Many banking apps break down expenses into different categories. Look at the details. For example, what restaurants are you going to? Maybe there are more fast-food restaurants than expected?

You can see your life in these numbers. You may be surprised how mistaken you are about your life. The life you think you are living may not be the life you are actually living. It's all there in the numbers.

If you find behaviors that don't match your goals or that don't match your identity, then use this time to figure out solutions.

Maybe you'll find you aren't working out as often as you thought. Perhaps you'll find you are eating a lot of hidden calories. Maybe you'll find you aren't getting enough sleep.

You can deal with whatever you find—once you are aware of it.

Don't Be Boring

Adding this habit to your daily check-in is a powerful way to keep your weight under control, but please don't think the point of this habit is to stop doing all the things you enjoy. That's not the purpose at all.

What's life without a bit of fun? It's boring; that's what it is. Don't be bored. Do what you want; just make sure you want it.

14. Habit: Play Big Goal Little Goal

Set short-term goals until you reach your long-term goal.

This is a game you can play when your brain tells you to stop. Let's say you have a big goal, completing 35 minutes on the treadmill. But after a while, you want to stop. A way to motivate yourself is to **set a smaller goal you can reach quickly**.

People do much better when they make regular progress toward a visible, well-defined goal.

For example, if you ask people to hold up their arm as long as they can, they'll hold it up for a much shorter time than when they are asked to hold their arm up for 10 minutes.

There's something about not having a specific goal that allows people to give up earlier.

So **make little goals.** Instead of thinking about your big goal, make a pact with yourself to reach a little goal, like just one more minute or just reaching one more blinking dot on the treadmill display. Whatever works for you.

To reach the little goal, you can *Bring Your Goal Picture to Mind*. When you get there, set another little goal. Keep setting little goals until you reach your big goal. Before you know it, you'll have reached your big goal without giving in to your unwanted thoughts of quitting.

You can change each little goal too. You can say I'll do this little goal at a sprint or a higher treadmill elevation. Change up anything to make it exciting and different.

I use this habit all the time. One of my favorite examples is a hike I take up this scary steep hill. Walking it is like inching up a flag pole. But it's not straight up. It undulates like a rock-armored snake. Each rise up the snake's back is about 100 yards. At the end of each rise is an arch, which levels off for a few yards. It repeats this pattern all the way to the top. Going up the hill is a constant cycle of hiking up the long rise, resting a little in the flats, tackling the next long rise, and praying for the next flat to finally come again.

To get through the hike, I make it a game of *Big Goal Little Goal*. The big goal is to get to the top. But five minutes into the hike, I am breathing hard and don't care about the big goal anymore. So I make a little goal of hitting the next flat. About halfway up a rise, I get so tired I quit caring about getting to the next flat part of the trail. Remember, this is a steep hill! So I make an even littler goal of just taking the next step. I eventually get to the top one step, one rise, and one flat at a time.

It's not heroic, but it works.

15. Habit: Make a Life

==Making an interesting life for yourself focuses your attention away from food.==

We have lots of open ground where we live and a massive weed problem. Some years it seems we are growing a weed garden instead of a real garden. We weed and weed, yet we can't keep up.

Then we discovered something interesting. Some of our plants could keep the weeds out all on their own. These plants are self-seeding, which means they spread and grow by themselves, so they crowd out the pesky weeds and don't give them any place to grow. We are growing more of these miracle plants in the hope that, over the long run, the weeds will never again be able to establish themselves in our garden.

Our relationship with food is similar to the plants that grow so well they crowd out the weeds.

Dr. Nora Volkow, director of the National Institute on Drug Abuse, thinks people are less likely to need the artificial boost of food and drugs if they create meaningful connections to the world. The more naturally excited about your life you are, the less you need other substitutes. Dr. Volkow says:

> **If you don't get excited by everyday things in life, if things look gray, and the drug makes things look extraordinary, that puts you at risk. But if you get great excitement out of a great multiplicity of things and intensely enjoy these things—seeing a movie, or climbing a mountain—and then you try a drug, you'll think: What's the big deal?**

Dr. Volkow bases her recipe for happiness on exciting new research on how our body decides what to pay attention to. Food isn't as potent as drugs, but it can still demand our attention when there aren't other interests to crowd out the thoughts of food.

Food won't seem so important if we can give ourselves something else to pay attention to.

She is asking us something we all want for ourselves but is still hard to do: for us to have **interesting lives.**

The "Rat Park" experiments conducted in the 1970s by Dr. Bruce Alexander shows the wisdom of Dr. Volkow's often difficult-to-follow advice. Dr. Alexander and his research team thought rats became addicted to drugs in experiments because the rats had **awful lives.** They lived lonely lives in isolated wire cages.

To prove their idea, they created Rat Park, 200 square feet of rat heaven featuring bright balls, tin cans to play with, painted creeks and trees, and plenty of space for mating and socializing. The rats were given access to the same sweet morphine-laced drinks. Another group of cage-bound rats were given access to sweet morphine-laced drinks.

What the researchers found was surprising, especially if you, as I did, thought all the rats would become equally addicted to the morphine drink. After all, it's morphine; wouldn't any rat be attracted to the constant stream of morphine-induced pleasure? Curiously, the answer is no.

Rats living in Rat Park had so much fun they barely touched their sweet morphine cocktail. In contrast, rats stuck in isolated cages eagerly drank more than a dozen times the amount of morphine solution as the rats in the park.

The implication is clear: **living unhappy and disconnected lives encourages addiction**.

A sunflower turns toward the bright sun as it grows. If you don't have something bright in your life, you may turn toward the darkness.

16. Habit: Create Your Support Group

A support system can make you more than twice as likely to maintain your weight loss.

One of the reasons I like to see movies is because they remind me of thoughts and feelings that get lost in the repetition of daily life. I get busy, and my attention narrows down to just the stuff I need to do to get through the day.

Seeing a good comedy reminds me to laugh. Seeing a good drama reminds me to find a deeper meaning in life. Movies reconnect me with parts of life that are easily lost without a little reminder.

A support system is like watching a movie for controlling your weight. A support system keeps your mind focused on controlling your weight. Otherwise, you are likely to forget and drift back into old habits that never worked in the first place. Doing something, almost anything consistently will help keep you on target.

Keeping you involved may be the secret of why support systems work so well. Studies show **a support system can make you more than twice as likely to maintain your weight loss.**

That's a powerful force to have working on your side. And that's why you should think seriously about making a support system as one of your habits.

Internet-based support systems can be as effective as a structured group or one-on-one in-person support programs. Pick whatever form of support you think will work best for you. Weight Watchers, for example, has excellent in-person support groups. And there are a bunch of support communities online for you to choose from.

When looking for a support system, think about what kind of support has worked for you in the past. Do you want to bounce ideas off people? Do you want people to share with? Do you want encouragement? Are you looking for great recipes? Do you need help with goal setting? Are you looking for role models? Are you looking for a positive environment? Do you want education and mentoring? Do you want daily email reminders? Would online food, calorie, and exercise tracking help you?

Figure out what will help to keep you on target the best.

17. Habit: Look Good Now

Don't wait to buy nice clothes. Looking your best at all times helps transform you inside and out.

Many people wait to buy new clothes until they've reached their goal weight. While this is understandable, don't wait. Buy clothes that fit you now. Look your best at all times. That includes both during the weight loss process and if you are gaining weight.

If you squeeze into your old clothes, you will just feel sad and bad. If you are wearing your old baggy clothes while losing weight, then you are keeping your old self around instead of building up your new self.

Clothes can make a fantastic difference in how you feel about yourself. Your chances of staying on a diet are much higher if you feel good about yourself and your direction.

What Not to Wear Shows the Power of Clothes

The immense power of this habit was brought home to me by watching the TV show *What Not to Wear* on BBC. In *What Not to Wear*, hosts Trinny and Susannah, a pair of brutally honest fashion writers, select a woman (and sometimes a man) who her friends and family have nominated as needing a complete style makeover.

The contestant is given about $4,000 to buy a completely new wardrobe. All her old clothes are thrown away. It's a fresh start.

The hosts don't just give her money and tell her to go shopping. They give her a set of rules about what clothes will look best on her and why. The rules teach her how to look the best she possibly can, given her strengths and weaknesses. For the rest of her life, she'll know how to buy clothes that make her look her best.

You might think this show is mainly about fashion and clothes, and it is about those too. It's about the **inner transformation** these women must undergo before they accept that they can be attractive, vibrant women again.

Having reached a comfort zone with their clothes and lives, they usually resist any change, even though it's obvious to everyone around them that they could look so much better. And at the end of the show, they usually **look and feel astonishingly better.**

The before and after shots are dramatic. Selecting clothes that hide what needs hiding and emphasizing each woman's strengths makes a stunning difference.

What's clear from watching the show is that these women were never really as bland as their before picture. They had just given up and needed Trinny and Susannah's tough love and excellent advice to get going again.

We hide behind our clothes. We become invisible because we don't think we deserve any better. We lack confidence. We think looking better is impossible for us. *What Not to Wear* shows that's not true

At the end of each episode, it's not the change of clothes we notice but the difference in the women we notice. We see them smiling and happy, strong and confident, amazed at how much better they look. We see them with hope.

That's the transformation proper fitting and well-styled clothes can help to make in you.

This was a tough habit for me. I've never paid much attention to clothes. I never liked clothes, and I hated shopping for them.

But *What Not to Wear* made a significant impact on me. Seeing these women bloom motivated me to give dressing better a try.

And I do try now. I've upgraded my wardrobe, and I feel a difference inside. I feel more confident in myself. But I still hate shopping!

18. Habit: Manage Your Stress

Reduce your constant desire to eat more fat and sugar by managing stress.

Humans love the right amount of stress. Stress energizes, stimulates, and excites. That's why people go on wild rides at the amusement park, watch horror movies, crank up the music or go a little too fast on the freeway. The goal is not to have a stress-free life. A little bit of stress is fun.

And that's what you are built to handle: a little bit of stress at a time.

Historically, stress did come in short bursts. Let's say it's late at night, and suddenly you see someone possibly lurking outside your window. To respond to the threat, your body immediately mobilizes all its resources and shuts down everything nonessential. You release energy so you can either fight or flee. Your heart rate goes up. You start to sweat. Your pupils dilate. Your body turns off growth, digestion, reproduction, and your immune system, so you save energy. There's no reason to worry about reproduction in a crisis. You need to worry about surviving. Now!

All these physical responses turn on when you think something threatening is happening. The threat doesn't have to be real. You just have to think it is. If the stranger turns out to be a burglar, you are prepared. But let's say the scary stranger is really your roommate. Then your thinking immediately changes. You sigh with relief, and all the physical stress responses reverse, and you go back to normal again.

That's exactly how your stress response is supposed to work. Stress stays low normally, a crisis happens, and your stress response ramps up, and once the crisis is over, you return to normal.

Chronic Stress Decreases Your Life Expectancy

The problem is that in the modern world, you can experience stress all the time. You may experience stress in traffic, waiting in line at the grocery store, or worrying about your mortgage. The number of stressors in modern life is potentially infinite.

All these are psychological stresses. They **come from your belief** that something threatening is happening. You think yourself into feeling stressed. The good news is that you can learn to manage these stresses.

Psychological stresses, like worrying about being fired from your job, can be chronic, which means they happen all the time. The problem is that your stress response is not meant to be on all the time.

When you suffer chronic stress, all those wonderful fight or flight responses start causing damage, and you get sick. You can suffer from hypertension, impotence, osteoporosis, exhaustion, muscle wasting, ulcers, heart disease, and memory loss. Chronic stress is not good for you.

What can you do about chronic stress?

Dealing with stress is a lot like dealing with weight problems. Stress management isn't something you can fit into a five-minute break between meetings or just do on the weekends. It's something you have to do all the time, which is exactly like staying on a diet, and that is why managing stress and staying on a diet are both so hard.

Some common stress management techniques are:

- **Relaxation Exercises**. You relax muscle groups throughout your body. When a stressful event happens, you can use this skill to reduce tension.

- **Breathing Exercises**. You breathe deeply when you become stressed like you do when you are calm so that you can control your fight-flight response.
- **Meditation**. Meditation is a skill that has been shown to be very calming and improves your ability to handle stress.
- **Visual Imagery**. You take time during the day to imagine being in a pleasant and calming place.
- **Physical Exercise**. Exercise helps to relieve stress and improves your physical, emotional, and mental health.
- **Positive Self-talk**. Talk to yourself with positive, calming phrases like "I am calm, I can stay relaxed," "Breathe deeply and slowly, let the tension go," or "I can handle this." Too often, the way we talk to ourselves inside our own heads just makes things worse.
- **Balanced, Healthy Lifestyle**. Eat a balanced diet, get enough sleep, don't work too much, have fun, develop meaningful relationships, and put some effort into spiritual growth.
- **Avoid Alcohol and Drugs to Cope With Stress**. You only create more stress by using drugs and alcohol.

All these techniques can work well for you. But in the end, these are all just rules. What is hard is consistently applying them. Overcoming temptation is always a challenge.

To go beyond techniques, you have to look at attitudes. Why does one person get stressed in a traffic jam, and another sing along with the radio, apparently unaffected by the traffic disaster around them?

What makes the same exact event psychologically stressful for one person and not another? Why does one person see the glass as half-full and another person see the glass as half-empty? It stands to reason that if you can be more like the people who handle stress better, then you can avoid the bad effects of chronic stress.

The Long-Lived Nuns

A fascinating study called the *Nun Study* shows how certain personality traits help some people handle stress better, and that handling stress leads to much better health as you age.

Data has been collected from the School Sisters of Notre Dame for over thirty years. Nuns are an excellent group to study because they live in very similar environments over long periods of time.

Researchers noticed that the nuns who had the most positive attitude at a very young age were twice as likely to be alive late in life compared to sisters who were more negative at a young age. That's a dramatic difference.

The nuns who aged well showed a sense of humor and the ability to adapt to new challenges. It's not that these nuns didn't experience psychological stress. They did. But because of their positive attitude, it's thought they **shut down their stress response sooner** and quickly returned to normal. They didn't experience chronic stress.

So the obvious next question is: how do you get a better attitude?

Develop a Better Stress-Handling Attitude

Robert M. Sapolsky, a top stress researcher, has come up with a few characteristics of better stress handlers:

- **Can you tell the difference between a big thing and a little thing?** A lion attacking you is a big thing. Is a traffic jam really a big thing, or is it more likely a little thing? Better stress handlers know which is a real threat.
- **If it's a big thing, do you try to get a little control?** Do you take control by acting, or do you just sit around and mope? Better stress handlers don't sit passively by and let events happen to them. They try to get some control of a situation by acting.
- **Can you tell if the outcome is good or bad?** Can you tell when your life is improving? Can you tell when you've won or lost? Or do you get just as stressed over a good outcome as a bad outcome? Better stress handlers can tell when they've won, and there's no reason to be stressed anymore.

- **If the outcome is bad, do you at least have an outlet for dealing with the stress?** Do you take your frustration out in other ways or just bottle it up? Better stress handlers find a way to release their pent-up emotions rather than keep them inside.

Approaching events in your life with these steps in mind will help you become a better stress handler.

Develop a Supportive Social Network

Unfortunately, it won't be enough to manage stress using only the stress management techniques we talked about earlier. Neither is developing a better stress-handling attitude. There's a much bigger source of stress in your life that we have yet to discuss: **isolation.**

Sapolsky says you are much more likely to have high-stress levels if you are socially isolated. There is a **threefold difference in mortality rates** for people who are socially isolated.

Being alone is a major source of stress. This is especially true as you age. As you age, the people in your life may get sick, grow apart or die. Many older people find themselves all alone, which is a major health risk for them.

Humans are social animals. A big part of our well-being seems to come from connections to other people. It's crucial to keep and develop relationships with family and friends, especially as you age.

19. Habit: Sleep Better

Sleep is the best nootropic, stress relief, trauma release, immune booster, hormone augmenter, and emotional stabilizer.

Sleep is likely the single best thing you can do to reset your body and health. You may not be aware, but sleep also plays a key role in weight management.

People who sleep better consume **about 270 fewer calories** a day than chronically sleep-deprived people. That's 26 pounds over three years!

You need a good night's sleep. How?

According to Andrew Huberman, Ph.D., a neuroscientist and tenured Professor in the Department of Neurobiology at the Stanford University School of Medicine, here's how you get your best night's sleep:

- View sunlight for at least 20 minutes by going outside within 30-60 minutes of waking.
- View sunlight again before sunset.
- Wake up at the same time each day and go to sleep when you first start to feel sleepy.
- Avoid caffeine within 8-10 hours of bedtime.
- Avoid viewing bright lights, especially overhead lights, between 10 pm and 4 am.
- Limit daytime naps to less than 90 min, or don't nap at all.
- If you have sleep disturbances, insomnia, or sleep anxiety, try some form of self-hypnosis.
- Expect to feel really alert about 1 hour before your natural bedtime. This is natural. It will pass.
- If you wake up in the middle of the night, try a Non-Sleep Deep Rest (NSDR) script. See the chapter on Max Workout for an NSDR meditation.
- Keep the room you sleep in cool and dark, and layer on blankets you can remove.
- Drinking alcohol interferes with your sleep, as do most sleep medications.

- Consider taking before bed: 145mg Magnesium Threonate or 200mg Magnesium Bisglycinate; 50mg Apigenin; 100-400mg Theanine.

20. Habit: Daily Reminders

> **If you don't think about staying on your diet regularly, then you probably won't.**

It takes me only a couple of days to slide out of my good habits and back into the bad ones. How long does it take for you? Not very long, either?

A recent study showed that people who got daily diet reminder emails had a BMI lower than those who didn't. That helps to validate the idea that you need to be continually involved with staying on your diet, or you'll fall off.

How can you build into your life the mindfulness needed to control your weight?

- **Keep a Journal.** People who regularly keep a journal have been found to maintain their weight loss better.
- **Sign Up for Mindful Email.** A mindful email service sends you a daily email with helpful suggestions on controlling your weight. It's not really the suggestion that helps, though it may; it's more the reminder that keeps you aware of your need to control your weight. Researchers at the University of Alberta in Edmonton have shown that emails promoting healthier eating and increased physical activity reduce people's weight.
- **Participate in On-line Groups.** Talking with other people in online groups keeps you involved in your diet.
- **Join a Challenge.** Challenges kick in your competitive spirit to help you lose weight. You may, for example, choose to participate in a "steps challenge," where you and a group of like-minded adventurers devise your daily step goal and track the number of steps you take each day. You might like a "vegetable challenge," where you are asked to creatively include more vegetables in your daily meals. The most common challenge is the "weight loss challenge," where you challenge yourself to lose a certain amount of weight in a certain amount of time. You might even compete against others to see who can hit their weight loss target. What makes challenges fun

is your built-in support community. Challenge participants get together to talk about different ideas and help each other. More and more challenges are being created all the time.

21. Habit: Leverage Your Metabolism

Muscles continuously burn calories so you can eat more and still lose weight.

The difference between losing and gaining weight can be just a few hundred calories a day. If you could change something about your body to burn a few hundred more calories a day, would you?

Excellent! You can burn more calories by building muscle through weight lifting. You knew there had to be a catch, didn't you?

Adding muscle increases your resting metabolism. These are the calories you burn when you are doing nothing and when you are absolutely at rest.

Your brain, for example, is only about 2% of your weight but consumes about 20% of your total energy! Your body must burn calories to run your brain, even when you aren't doing anything. And it's the same for every other part of your body. Running your body takes a lot of calories.

If you have a faster metabolism, you burn more calories and store less fat. If you have a slower metabolism, you burn calories less efficiently and therefore store more calories as fat. You want your metabolism always working for you, burning more calories and keeping you out of starvation mode.

Your resting metabolism is responsible for 50–75% of the calories you burn each day. Digestion accounts for about 10%, and physical activity for 15–40%.

What is the single biggest calorie burner in your resting metabolism? Your muscles. **Simply by building muscle and becoming more active, you can increase your resting metabolic rate by 15% or more.**

This is why many men can seemingly eat all they want when they are younger and not gain weight. Men tend to have more muscle mass than women, so the extra food is burned up. But old age makes the sexes equal. As we age, we lose muscles, which is one of the reasons we gain weight as we grow older.

Replace Fat with Muscle to Lose Weight

How do you get a faster metabolism? By **replacing fat with muscle.**

One pound of fat burns about four calories a day. One pound of muscle burns a whopping 50 calories a day. So the more muscle you add, the more calories you burn.

The exciting benefit of burning calories by adding muscle is that you are burning these calories 24 hours a day without any extra effort on your part.

Muscle is like interest on your savings account. You earn interest on your money and don't have to do anything but let the money sit in your bank account. Muscle works the same way.

The more muscle you add, the more calories you burn, and the easier it is for you to lose weight. Another benefit of adding muscle is that when you reach your target weight, you can afford to eat more food because of all the extra calories your muscles are burning. You'll also feel stronger and happier, have more energy, and look better in clothes. What a deal! A free wonder drug. How can you not take it?

Creating Your Resistance Training Program

You've learned about many of the wonderful benefits of muscles, so how do you build them? With resistance or weight training! The key point is it's not as hard as you may think. We always hear about those hard-charging folks who spend hours in the gym. Fortunately, you can lift twice weekly for about 20 minutes each day and see significant results.

You'll see strong benefits if you can work weightlifting into your life.

22. Habit: Move to a Place Where You Will Naturally Be More Active

Move to a location where you will naturally walk more and drive less.

Imagine that you are thinking of moving and you are considering two different locations: *Sit City* and *Active Town*.

You like Sit City because you can buy a great house for a good price. But there are a few problems with Sit City. There are no sidewalks in the neighborhood you would be moving to, and you're concerned it would be hard to walk safely on the roads. There aren't any parks or schools close by so you couldn't walk there either. Your house is miles and miles away from a real town center; all you have close to you are strip malls. Strip malls mean most of your eating options are fast food restaurants, and you'll have to drive everywhere. And strip mall living means you won't have stores close by offering quality fresh fruits and vegetables at reasonable prices.

You can see what your life will be like in Sit City. You will eat bad food, drive everywhere, and sit inside your house all the time watching TV. Year after year, you can just see the pounds being packed on.

You really like Active Town, but it is more expensive, and the house is smaller. It's one of those new communities organized like older small town centers. Near your house is a mix of parks, shops, bike paths, golf courses, offices, and stores with fresh fruits and vegetables. You can walk or bike everywhere, and you hardly need to drive.

You can see what your life will be like in Active Town. You won't have the giant house you always dreamed of. That hurts a little. But your life will be better in most ways that matter, kind of like how small-town living used to be. There's a main street where you can shop for fresh food and parks to play. And you'll have a better chance of meeting people too.

Which place should you pick to live? In making your decision, you may want to consider the impact on your weight. You may not have thought about where you live as having a lot to do with your weight, but it does.

People who live in a community where they can walk to shop, work, eat and socialize have been found to be thinner.

The reason is simple: they walk more and drive less. A University of Maryland study found people who live in the most sprawling counties are the most likely to be overweight.

The best predictor of not being obese is, amazingly, having shops and services near where you live. The environment in which you live is the driving force for how much physical activity you'll naturally get in your daily life. Your environment also has a lot to do with the available quality and cost of food. In Sit City, you'll naturally get far less exercise and worse food than you would in Active Town.

If you currently live in a Sit City, **you may want to think about moving** to a place like Active Town. Some real estate listings provide a walkability score. Moving may seem extreme, but it may be the easiest way to create a situation where you will naturally walk more. Creating situations where you naturally walk more is the core of creating effective habits.

Just give moving some thought. You may find this one of the most effective strategies you could ever implement.

Active Towns are Being Built

Active Town is not a fictional place; well the name is fictional. Verrado, near Phoenix, Arizona, is one impressive example of an Active Town development. Their vision of the future is to re-create a modern version of the classic American small town instead of sprawling suburbs connected by overcrowded roads.

You'll find a small-town feel in Verrado. Many houses have front porches. There's a core downtown with a main street lined with shops, cafes, and restaurants. Open spaces are scattered throughout the development and are easy to walk from homes. Neighborhoods are walkable, and schools are close and accessible.

This is the kind of place where you'll want to walk, and that could make all the difference in controlling your weight. Verrado is not alone. Many communities like Verrado are now being built.

23. Habit: Take it Easy

You can't exercise if you get injured or sick, and you won't be able to control your weight.

A study supported by the National Heart, Lung, and Blood Institute shows that women trying to lose weight can benefit as much from moderate physical activity as from an intense workout. **It's more important for you to exercise regularly than to force hard exercise.**

For you hard chargers out there, this should be news you can use. You don't need to kill yourself, especially as you grow older.

How many times have you pushed and injured yourself? It can take months to come back from a pulled muscle. Tendonitis, a classic overuse injury, can take years to clear up. Ignoring a cold can add weeks and weeks to the time you're sick.

So use your judgment. It's much more important that you keep exercising over time than it is for you to give it all you have one week and then nurse an injury for the next few months.

This is a very hard lesson to learn for competitive people. You've spent your entire life pushing and pushing and pushing some more. And there comes a time your body starts pushing back. This time comes for everyone, even you.

If you are in doubt, wait it out. Avoid injuries. Nothing stops an exercise program faster than getting hurt. You can't exercise if you are injured, so be careful out there.

24. Habit: Walk the Walk

You can find more steps to take almost anywhere, anytime. Every additional step adds up to more calories burned.

Walking is the king of all exercise because it is free, available, and good for your health. Walking requires no equipment, can be done almost anywhere, lowers blood pressure, shapes and tones your body, burns calories, strengthens back muscles, reduces the risk of heart disease and diabetes, and reduces stress.

I've read that if walking were a drug, it would be the most prescribed drug on earth.

We, humans, are world-class walkers. Our ancestors walked miles each day to hunt and gather food. You have this incredible innate ability to walk much longer and farther than you think.

America on the Move is an organization dedicated to helping you exploit your walking genius for weight loss. Their initiative is to improve health and prevent obesity with a goal for each person to move more and eat less by making two small daily changes.

- Add an extra 2,000 steps (or activity equivalent) to your day. Two thousand steps is about one mile.
- Choose one smart way to eat 100 fewer calories each day. One hundred calories is about one tablespoon of butter.

If you implement both of these steps, you will prevent the current average American weight gain of 1–2 pounds a year.

The long-term goal of *America on the Move* is for **everyone to take a total of 10,000 steps a day,** which is approximately 5 miles. That's about how far our hunter-gatherer ancestors walked each day. Even an inactive person takes 1,000 to 3,000 steps a day.

Every little bit helps. Start with a few extra steps, and then add more as you can.

Start by using some sort of activity tracker (smart watch, step tracker, Fitbit, etc.) to get an idea of how many steps you take in a day on average.

Then make a goal of walking 2,000 more steps a day. If you can manage to do that, you are getting more exercise and burning more calories. After you reach your 2,000 steps, you can make an even higher goal.

At first, I thought this program was, well, silly. The idea of counting your steps rather than going running or something more substantial didn't seem useful to me. But I've totally changed my tune.

Now I seek extra steps everywhere. Thinking about adding a few extra steps wherever you can is a very powerful idea. And the extra steps really add up.

How much do all the extra steps add up to? That's why an activity tracker is useful. It's excellent feedback on how you're doing, and having a good source of feedback is critical for keeping any habit on target.

Measuring Activity Using Steps is Better than Using Time

Having a **goal of walking a certain number of steps** a day may be more effective than setting a goal of exercising a certain amount of time.

One study found the actual physical activity recorded was significantly lower for women whose goal was to exercise 30 minutes a day when compared to women who had a goal of reaching 10,000 steps a day.

The reason was that the women with a 10,000-step-a-day goal **would still come close to their goal,** even if they didn't quite reach it. Women who had a goal of exercising for 30 minutes may have had an all-or-nothing attitude that caused them to give up when they couldn't fit in their 30 minutes of exercise.

This study is an exciting confirmation of my own experience. When your goal is to get more steps each day, you can seize any opportunity to add more steps to your total. If your goal is to exercise for 30 minutes, it's all too easy just to skip it.

When I had a goal of adding an extra 2,000 steps a day, I started looking for all sorts of ways to add additional steps. Just having a goal makes a difference. Goals get your mind unconsciously plotting on your behalf.

Now I find more steps almost everywhere. I can take a longer path through the grocery store. I can get up from my desk at work and take a short walk. I can park farther away from entrances. I can take the stairs instead of an elevator. I can get up during TV commercials and march in place or take a little walk (it's a good way to avoid those tempting food commercials). Once you start looking, steps are everywhere for the taking.

Park Far Away from an Entrance

Don't park as close as you can to an entrance; park far away. You will naturally walk more.

Long ago, I heard the suggestion to park far away from entrances, and I rolled my eyes. How much of a difference could it really make? Then I decided to try parking far away from entrances.

It really works!

Now it's one of my favorite strategies because it's so simple, easy, and effective, and there are so many opportunities to use it. Think of all the times you park your car and enter a building. That's a lot of opportunities.

Let's run some numbers on this habit. When I park at work, for example, I park far enough away that I add a total of 400 additional steps (200 steps each way) to my daily total.

Now, let's say I park at five different places during the day, and each time I find 400 additional steps. Over a day, that's 2,000 extra steps!

That's an extra mile of walking from just this one simple habit.

25. Habit: Take the Stairs

Lose over 3 pounds a year by climbing up and down 5 flights of stairs a day.

An easy way to add a few more steps to your day is to take the stairs. Over a year you can easily lose 3 pounds using this one simple habit. You don't think it can be that much? Let's run some numbers.

You burn about 10 calories per minute going up a flight of stairs and 7 calories per minute going down. It takes about 2.5 minutes to climb 5 flights of stairs. It takes about 1 minute to descend them. When you add all that up, you burn 32 calories ascending and descending 5 flights of stairs.

If you can make this one simple change a day—ascending and descending 5 flights of stairs—you can burn off over 3 pounds a year! That's a lot of weight. It could be all you need to keep from becoming obese.

Most people don't take the stairs. Researchers found that only 6–9% of people chose to use the stairs instead of elevators or escalators. If they were aware of how many calories they could burn, maybe they might change their minds.

For a while, I worked on the fourth floor of an office building. I noticed that people who worked on the second floor used the stairs a lot of the time. Once you work on the third floor or above, forget it, you use the elevator.

When I first started working there, I was excited I would be able to use this habit. I could see the calories just dropping off as I happily climbed stairs every day. It didn't turn out exactly as I expected.

I was going up and down stairs 10 times a day! That's a lot of stairs to go up. I was getting tired and sweaty and neither is a good way to get ahead on your job. So I decided to modify my habit.

I decided I would aim to go up the stairs once or twice a day, depending on how I felt, and I would always go down the stairs. Most days I was able to go up the stairs twice and down the stairs 10 or so times.

That's still a lot of extra calories burned for one simple change.

26. Habit: Take Walking Meetings and Breaks

Find extra steps in your day by holding meetings while walking and during breaks. Every little walk adds extra steps.

Walk During Meetings

Not all meetings have to be held sitting down at a table under artificial lights. If you are talking, take a stroll in the hallways or, better yet, outside. You'll probably be more creative as exercise pumps up your brain.

Walk During Breaks

Get up every hour or so and take a short walk.

We weren't meant to stay in one place all day. By taking a short brisk walk, you increase the number of steps you are taking, reduce the chance of getting repetitive strain injury (RSI), and jump-start your brain so you'll be sharper during the day.

Put your walk break in your calendar so you'll remember to take it. Get a few other people in the office to walk with you so you can help each other remember. It may take some creativity to find a place to walk. You can walk the hallways if there is nowhere outside or the weather is uninviting.

27. Habit: Exercise in the Morning

Ninety percent of people who exercise consistently exercise in the morning.

The longer you put off exercise the less chance that you'll do it. You'll be tired, or something will come up.

Morning exercise has other benefits too. When you exercise in the morning, you'll feel energized for the day. Many people find they are less hungry after morning exercise. And many people think morning exercise puts them in a healthier mindset and helps them make better food choices throughout the day.

What really matters is developing an exercise habit. It doesn't really matter when you do it as long as you do it. But you may be more successful over the long run if you choose a morning workout time.

28. Habit: Work with a Personal Trainer

> **A personal trainer can help keep you on a schedule and force you to exercise, even when you don't want to.**

Many people work better when they are working with other people in accomplishing a goal. Going it alone can be hard. That's where working with a good personal trainer comes in.

Working with a personal trainer sets up a system of **accountability.** It's just natural to not want to disappoint your personal trainer so you are more likely to work harder and keep with the program.

A personal trainer also serves as a **mentor.** You'll learn a lot about being healthy. You'll learn about exercise, nutrition, and what it takes to make your exercise program a success.

When you are busy with life and everything is saying you don't have time to exercise, your personal trainer will be the one person **motivating** you and creating a positive environment in which you can succeed. Sometimes you just need an ally who supports your goals.

Even if you have never considered using a personal trainer, you may want to give one a chance. If you are shy or the cost of a trainer is a bit high, then maybe you and a few of your friends can share a personal trainer.

By hiring a personal trainer now, when you have the willpower, you are making it more likely you will exercise later, even when you don't feel like exercising. And that puts you in the best position to succeed.

29. Habit: Increase Your NEAT

Sit rather than lie down, stand rather than sit, and walk rather than stand. Find ways to move even a little bit more during the day.

Obese people naturally sit more than lean people. Fidgeters can burn 300–800 calories a day not from exercising, but from everyday activities.

Think about this: running 8 miles burns about 800 calories. By fidgeting, you could burn as many calories as running 8 miles!

How fidgety you are is called your NEAT (non-exercise activity thermogenesis) quotient. Even those of us not blessed with a high NEAT can consciously learn how to change our daily activity levels.

Your goal is to figure out little ways through which you can increase your NEAT. In the past, you may have felt like I did, that those little bits of activity didn't count, but it turns out they may be what counts most of all.

The increased calorie burn from fidgeting is amazing. Fidgeters, for example, burn 40–60 more calories per hour when seated than people who sit motionlessly. Standing fidgeters burn 70–100 calories more per hour than people who stand still. Those are big differences.

Here are some suggestions on how to become NEATer:

- Get up and out of your seat. Stand up instead of sitting down.
- You could lose one pound a year simply by sending one less email each hour. Instead, walk down the hall to talk to the person you would have sent the email to. That short walk burns off one pound a year.
- Laughing for 10 or 15 minutes burns about 50 calories. Laugh that much every day and you've lost 5 pounds in a year.
- Walking around instead of sitting while on the cell phone burns up to 50 calories in 10 minutes.
- Put a portable pedal exerciser in front of your TV and pedal slowly while you watch. You can do the same while reading.

- Put a treadmill in front of your computer at work. Every hour on the treadmill at 1 mph is about 100 calories.
- Pick a time each hour when you get up and take a little walk. Maybe go look out a window. Take a turn around your building. Go to the bathroom.
- Tap your feet. Wiggle your fingers.
- Performing sit-ups during commercials while watching TV burns up to 65 calories an hour.
- Dance while you cook.
- Watching TV while sitting down burns about 72 calories an hour. Do light housework while watching TV and you bump the calorie burn up to 216 calories per hour.
- Take walking meetings.
- Hold meetings while standing.
- Walk to the mailbox instead of driving.

These are just a few ideas. Take a look and see where you can add even a little more activity.

The general rule, even if you aren't a natural fidgeter, is:

Sit rather than lie down, stand rather than sit, and walk rather than stand.

30. Habit: The Integrative Workout

> **You can easily burn 500 calories a day through normal everyday activities.**

Lee Labrada, a former Mr. Universe, has written a book titled *The Lean Body Promise,* in which he advocates burning more calories through the activities you already do each day. To make this work, you need to get a feel for how many calories you burn in your daily activities:

- **Activities That Burn About 4 Calories per Minute:** calisthenics, slow cycling, light gardening, social golf, general housework, line dancing, table tennis, doubles tennis, and slow walking.

- **Activities That Burn About 7 Calories per Minute:** aerobics, basketball, baseball, moderate cycling, active dancing, football, racquetball, skiing, swimming, singles tennis, and brisk walking.
- **Activities That Burn About 10 Calories per Minute:** competitive basketball, fast cycling, strenuous dancing, competitive football, jogging, kickboxing, running, cross-country skiing, jumping rope, vigorous swimming, vigorous walking, heavy weight training.

These calorie burn numbers are just estimates. Your mileage may vary depending on how much you weigh, your metabolism, and how intensely you perform an activity. A good general rule is to figure out your **normal everyday activities to burn about 7 calories a minute.** If you aren't sure if the physical activity you are performing is 4, 7, or 10 calories a minute, then run your calorie burn calculations using seven calories per minute.

You can use this information to create your own integrative workout.

Your goal is to find between 1 to 1.5 hours of physical activity and integrate it into your daily routine. Here's an example of an integrative workout routine from Mr. Labrada:

- **Monday:** to burn 500 calories: carry your child, vacuum, do other house cleaning chores, carry and

put the groceries away, run up and down stairs, squat, and lunge.
- **Tuesday:** to burn 600 calories: run up and down stairs, walk to the store, clean windows, and play with the kids.
- **Wednesday:** to burn 750 calories: walk the dog, play with kids, sweep the driveway, carry baby, run up and down stairs, squat, and lunge.
- **Thursday:** to burn 700 calories: push a stroller through the park, play with kids, vacuum, mop floors, carry laundry up and down the stairs, and run to the mailbox and back.
- **Friday:** to burn 800 calories: run errands on foot, walk your dog, carry baby, do lunges and squats, carry and unpack purchases, and play with kids.
- **Saturday:** to burn 500 calories: wash the car, walk to the store, play with kids on the playground, and work in the garden.
- **Sunday:** to burn 675 calories total: walk through the park, swim, and play with the kids.

What are the results? Let's add up the calories. It looks like you'll burn 4,525 calories a week on this plan, which is a weight loss of over one pound a week. That's a remarkable result from everyday activities you may not have thought about as burning a lot of calories.

Of course, you may not have a child to carry, but the general idea is sound. You just need to figure out replacement activities that fit your life.

For example, if you spend two hours in the mall searching for that perfect shirt, you'll have burned about 500 calories. A half-hour of shoveling snow off your sidewalk burns about 350 calories. An hour of raking leaves burns about 200 calories. Walking around your neighborhood looking at Christmas lights burns off a lot of calories too. When you are on the phone, walk around instead of sitting. Carry in groceries one bag at a time.

With a little creativity, you can find more exercise almost everywhere. And as we have seen, the calorie burn numbers are not trivial. Searching out and finding more physical activity in your daily life is a very rewarding weight loss move.

31. Habit: The Playground Workout

You can get a good workout from playing with your kids in the park.

Getting a workout while playing with your kids is fun and effective. You burn calories, work your muscles, and have a good time. Doesn't that sound better than exercising? Plus, you are spending quality time with your kids.

Here are some of the possible playground exercises:

- **Swings.** Pushing someone on a swing is like a mini chest press. It works your triceps, chest, and upper back. You burn about 50 calories in 10 minutes.

- **Slide.** Helping your child on the slide works your calves and back. You burn about 50 calories in 10 minutes. Don't be shy; go down the slide yourself too!
- **Merry-go-round.** This dizzying delight works your legs, butt, and back as you push your kids around in circles. You burn about 75 calories in 10 minutes.
- **Monkey-bars.** Hanging and climbing on the monkey bars works your abdominals, biceps, and upper back. You burn about 75 calories in 12 minutes.
- **Throw and catch.** Playing catch works your arms, shoulder, and lower back. You burn about 50 calories in 5 minutes.

The important idea here is to integrate exercise into your daily life if you look for opportunities. Before researching the Playground Workout, I wouldn't have thought about this venue for increasing fitness.

Thinking about play as exercise can sometimes give you that extra push you need to go out and have fun. We get so wrapped in life that taking time out for play, even with our children, may seem a frivolous waste of time. Now, in the back of your mind, you can think that you aren't just having fun, but you are burning calories and building muscles at the same time. Maybe just that little bit of motivation is all you need to get moving.

32. Habit: Just Don't Sit, Sit Actively

You can burn up to 350 calories daily by changing how you sit.

Office workers face a real problem getting more physical activity into their daily lives. They spend hour after hour sitting at a desk. What if you could turn sitting into exercise that could burn up to 350 calories daily?

Sit on an Exercise Ball

Sounds good, doesn't it? Sitting can be made to burn calories by using an **exercise ball** as your desk chair instead of a more traditional chair. In fact, as I am writing this sentence, I am sitting on an exercise ball instead of a regular chair.

Sitting on an exercise ball burns calories because it is an **unstable surface.** The ball is round and mushy, so you sink into it a little. You can't stay in one place without constantly using your muscles to keep balanced on top of the ball. That's why sitting on an exercise ball is called **active sitting.** You are actively engaging your abdominal and back muscles to keep them balanced.

Contrast active sitting to a traditional chair where you sit passively. The chair completely supports you, and you need minimal effort to sit. With active sitting, you aren't even aware you are burning calories; it's just a side effect of trying to stay balanced on the ball.

Exercise balls aren't for everyone. They take a bit of getting used to at first. They can also be tiring because you use muscle power to stabilize the ball. Start using your exercise ball as a chair in short chunks, slowly building up to using it all day.

Don't think exercise balls are just for work. You can use them everywhere. We have used exercise balls as chairs on our deck and for chairs at our dinner table. You could even have a house rule saying you can only watch TV while sitting on an exercise ball. Such a policy transforms passive TV viewing into a calorie-burning exercise!

Perform Soleus Pushups

What if you prefer sitting on a normal chair? You still have a great option. It's called the soleus pushup. Here's how you do it:

- Sit down.
- Hold your knees at approximately a 90-degree angle.
- Raise your heels off the ground while your toes are on the floor.
- Bring the heel down.
- Repeat for hours.

I know this sounds silly, but scientific research shows it improves glucose regulation and metabolism.

33. Habit: Exercise More in Zone 2

Exercise doesn't have to be hard.

Zone 2 is aerobic training for longer periods at a lower intensity.

Zone 2 training is exercising at 60 percent to 70 percent of your maximum heart rate. You want to exercise at a comfortable pace where you're right on the edge of being able to hold a conversation. It's your highest output while still being able to maintain a conversation.

It's a big switch in thinking, as the Zone 2 training pace is much slower than you're probably used to, which is why it's such a valuable form of exercise.

Many people won't exercise because they think it's too hard. Zone 2 changes that. Working out in Zone 2 is effective; it's not hard on your body, and you can do it for the rest of your life. Give it a try.

What are the advantages of Zone 2 training?

- Zone 2 burns more fat than any other form of exercise. If you have a lot of weight to lose, try Zone 2 training.
- The more Zone 2 training you do, the better you can uptake glucose, improve insulin sensitivity, and become more carbohydrate resistant.
- Zone 2 improves your ability to counteract damaging processes due to inflammation, which is often the result of excess fat.
- Zone 2 training improves your muscle's mitochondrial function by increasing its metabolic efficiency and capacity to burn fuel—fat, glucose, lactate—for energy. This optimizes your metabolic health and heals metabolic dysfunction.
- A common thread in Type 2 diabetes, obesity, cardiovascular disease, and Alzheimer's is mitochondrial dysfunction.
- Mitochondrial dysfunction is when your mitochondria are not working properly or as efficiently as they could be. When mitochondria are

not working correctly, we cannot burn glucose, which builds up in the blood.
- When excess glucose builds up, it can lead to all the problems mentioned earlier. Managing glucose through diet and exercise is crucial for increasing longevity.

What exercises can you do?

- Pick an activity like a treadmill, elliptical, rower, or stationary bike, where you can maintain a slow and steady pace for a long period. Biking or running outside may make maintaining a Zone 2 pace challenging because of the uphill or downhill sections. Remember, you don't want to slip into burning glucose. You want to burn fat for fuel, requiring a Zone 2 pace.
- All you need to do is walk an hour a day to keep your mitochondria healthy, especially if you want to eat more carbohydrates.

How often should you work out?

- Are you not in good condition? Start at 30 minutes three times a week.

- Zone 2, two days a week, is effectively a maintenance dose. You may not see improvement, but you'll arrest any decline.
- Zone 2, three days a week, starts to move the needle on improving your health.
- Zone 2, four days a week, 1 hour - 1.5 hours per day, is an ideal target for someone who is not just starting and is not an elite athlete.
- Zone 2, five days a week, is necessary for elite athletes to show improvement.

How long should you work out?

- Short intervals are not as effective as longer intervals.
- A Zone 2 session should be a minimum of 45 minutes, with 60-90 minutes being an ideal target.
- Remember, your heart rate target may increase as you get more fit.

When should you work out?

- Zone 2 training, because of its relatively slow pace, is perfect for doing with other activities you enjoy. I love to read during Zone 2 training on my elliptical machine. Other people listen to podcasts. Others make their Zone 2 training the only time they can watch TV. It's a tremendous complementary habit.

34. Habit: Go On the Dog Diet

Your dog needs walking, and so do you—a perfect match.

Every morning our two dogs, Annie and Stout, get restless. They want to go for their walk. Every time I go in the direction of the front door, Annie races ahead of me, thinking it's walk time. And when I don't open the door, I can see the excitement whoosh right out of her.

Later in the day, Annie will get more and more direct. She'll just come up in front of me, sit down, and stare. I know what she wants. She knows I know what she wants. The question is: will I go for a walk?

Even if I wasn't planning on it, the dogs could encourage and cajole me into going because they are just so darn cute and excited. Their energy is contagious, making me want to go even when I feel a little down.

No, that's not quite it. The dogs help me walk, especially when I am in one of those "I don't want to do anything" moods. It takes a hard person to ignore their "go on a walk dance" day after day.

So, you may want to consider getting a dog. Of course, you should only do so if you can commit to taking care of a dog, but if you can, a dog will help keep you active.

This habit isn't all just fanciful tales of puppy dog tails. There's real science behind it too.

A University of Missouri-Columbia study found **walking a dog can help you lose more weight in a year than most diet plans.** Dog walkers in the study averaged a weight loss of 14 pounds a year. If you can't see yourself getting a dog, maybe you can become a dog walker or volunteer at a dog shelter.

And dogs don't just help you get more exercise. They will be more than happy to help control your portion sizes by eating your leftovers!

35. Habit: Decide Exactly How Much You'll Eat Before Taking the First Bite

> **Create situations in which you won't eat more than you should. You can't trust your body to tell you when to stop eating.**

Has something like this happened to you? It's been a long day, and you're excited to take a break and go see a new movie. You buy a giant bag of popcorn, a large soda, and a box of candy—your usual. You could have purchased the small popcorn, but the giant bag was only a dollar more and came with free refills. Who can pass up that deal?

About halfway through the movie, you notice that all the popcorn is gone. How did that happen? You don't remember eating it all. Well, it happened one handful at a time. You think about how many calories you just ate, and you are amazed. A large bag of movie popcorn has about 1,700 calories. A large soda has about 1,200. A large box of candy has about 900 calories. Oh boy. That's almost two days' worth of calories in one sitting!

You may not have intended to eat everything. You may have intended to eat just part of the popcorn, or the candy, or the soda, but once you are in the middle of eating, it's almost impossible to stop.

That's why the goal of this habit is for you to **decide how much you'll eat before you start eating** and only have that amount of food in front of you. Follow this one rule, and your chances of overeating nose-dive. It's hard to eat food that isn't there.

You can always choose to eat more. Sometimes we consciously make that choice. No problem. We like food. We want to have fun but **consciously make the choice to overeat**. Don't let how much food happens to be served on your plate dictate how much you eat.

It's tempting to romanticize your body and think that if you could learn to live in harmony with it, all would be well. You could become a *natural* eater, and your weight would naturally stabilize at a nice slim and trim level.

Is something in our lives driving us to overeat? Are we overeating to fill the hole in our souls? Is it shame? Anxiety? Fear? Insecurity? Or some other deep psychological need?

Maybe. That's something reasonable to pursue. And I have no doubt it works for some people. And these people may think it will work for everyone else. But it doesn't work for me. It may not work for you either.

I can eat a whole cake, and my body is whispering *good job* the entire time. That's what "natural" means for me. My body is happy I found a good source of food; it loves eating as much as possible just in case I don't get to eat for a couple of days. If I ate what I "naturally" felt like, I would do nothing but gain weight.

Don't get me wrong; I would love to be a natural eater. And if natural eating works for you, then go for it. Whatever works. But don't expect natural eating to work; if it doesn't, don't feel like you are broken. We are all different, and not being a "natural" eater is part of your uniqueness.

To implement this habit, follow two steps:

- **Decide how much to eat.** Make your decision at the beginning of a meal because that's when your long-term thinking is at its strongest.
- **Get rid of the food you don't want.** Put away the food you don't want to eat or put it in a doggy bag **before** you start eating.

36. Habit: Eat Joyfully

One bite is enough.

Joyful Eating is an exciting new tasting technique I developed for experiencing peak pleasure from every glorious bite of food. It's based on a great deal of research into how our sense of taste works and, as you might imagine, a lot of enjoyable experimentation!

Joyful Eating helped me stay on my diet. How could a method of tasting food make such a big difference in my life?

Most weight loss diets feature denial as their key element. To lose weight, you are supposed to deny yourself certain foods—usually those you love the most—forever.

The problem is it's tortuously hard to stay on a diet over the long run by denying yourself the foods you love. Food is fun. Food is an excellent source of joy in life. The loss of joy is one of the biggest reasons diets fail.

For many, it simply isn't worth it. **Being thin doesn't feel better than how food tastes.** That's why so many people would rather feel the pleasure of food than stick to a denial-based diet.

Weight loss isn't the only reason people deny themselves the foods they love. Many people are on **health-restricted** diets as part of their treatment.

As a diabetic, for example, I avoid high-carbohydrate foods. People with heart conditions, high blood pressure, and many other diseases must watch what they eat too. Many feel like outcasts when they can't eat what other people are eating. It's often easier just to give in and eat everything.

How could you have the best of both worlds? How could you fully enjoy food while sticking to your diet? That's what Joyful Eating does for you.

By reveling in the power of food, Joyful Eating allows you to eat as little as one bite and feel satisfied. That's why Joyful Eating—tasting to its fullest—is one of the **secrets of eating in moderation.** You can feel more satisfaction from perfectly tasting a few bites of genuinely excellent food than from mindlessly eating a truck full of junk.

Clearly, if you have an allergy or your doctor says you should never eat certain foods, don't use Joyful Eating for those. But maybe you can use Joyful Eating for others.

I will never eat a whole piece of cake for the rest of my life. It would send my blood sugar numbers to the moon. But I can safely eat one glorious, perfect bite of cake.

The trick is learning how to extract enough pleasure from that one bite so that I will feel satisfied enough not to eat more.

Joyful Eating teaches you how to make one bite enough. One bite of anything won't have too many calories or other bad things, so it should be safe. And if you can stop eating after one bite, you will lose weight.

Joyful Eating works for any food. Use it for dessert, bread, potatoes, or whatever else you must be careful about eating. You can eat one, two, or even three bites and feel satisfied.

This approach works so well because your sense of taste is designed to make it work. Your brain encourages you to eat a variety of foods by dialing down the taste after a few bites. You actually stop tasting a flavor after just a few bites.

So why eat more than a couple of bites when you don't taste it? Why not spend your calorie budget on foods you can enjoy? If you can learn to extract the most pleasure from those few bites, you've learned to eat any food in moderation while still feeling satisfied. You've maximized pleasure while minimizing calories.

This is incredibly powerful, potentially **life-changing** stuff. At least, it was for me.

You can eat all the foods you love in moderation using Joyful Eating. You can go anywhere with anyone and not feel like an outcast. You don't have to abandon your health-restricted diet to feel like a real person again. And you will enjoy yourself more than you ever have before.

Joyful Eating is a **whole new kind of eating experience.** Perhaps for the first time in your life, you will have wholly tasted food with all your senses, including your most important sensory organ: **your mind.** Food will have never tasted so good.

The Joyful Eating practice has been carefully constructed to maximize the available sensory information to your brain. The more stimulation you get from your senses, the more satisfying any food will be. The more satisfying a food is, the less you need to eat of it. This is why there is such an emphasis on getting all your senses, including your mind, involved in the tasting process.

6 Steps to Joyful Eating

Here are the six steps to follow when eating joyfully. Tasting a raisin is used as an example, but any food will do.

Step 1: Clear Your Palate and Your Mind

- Clear your taste buds by taking a drink of room-temperature water.
- Wait at least 90 seconds for any previous tastes to fade away. While waiting, you can perform the following steps:
- Clear your mind of any preconceived ideas of how the raisin should taste. Discover the taste anew every time you eat.
- Give thanks for the raisin you are about to eat. Truly appreciate how special the opportunity to be alive to eat this raisin at this time.
- Take a deep breath. On a long exhale, let all the tension flow out of your body.
- Give yourself permission to enjoy yourself. Allow yourself to have fun.
- Bring to mind any pleasant memories of raisins or from similar situations in the past.
- Actively seek new tastes and experiences with your mind and senses as you eat. Find something new in every bite.
- Take your time. Don't rush.

Step 2: Get to Know Your Food with Your Senses

We'll explore how to taste using your sense of sight, touch, and smell.

Using sight...

- Place the raisin in the palm of your hand.
- And as you become aware of the weight of the raisin in your hand, carefully look at it as if you have never seen a raisin before.
- Ask yourself, what does the raisin look like? How does it compare to other things you have seen before? Appreciate its color and texture.
- Become aware of the different colors in the raisin. Are some rich? Are some light? Are some dark?
- And as you are feeling the raisin, hold it up to a light. Become aware of how the light shines on the raisin. Notice the highlights… the darker hollows and folds…explore every part of the raisin…as if you had never seen a raisin before.

Using touch...

- Become aware of how the raisin feels.
- Turn the raisin over between your fingers.

- And as you feel the pressure of the raisin on your fingers, explore its texture using your fingers and your entire hand.
- Ask yourself, what does the raisin feel like as it touches your fingers? Does it feel wet, dry, or sticky?
- How does it compare to other things you have felt before?

Using smell...

- Now bring the raisin close to your nose and take three short sniffs.
- What do you smell? What does the raisin smell like?
- How does it compare to other smells you remember?
- How powerful are the aromas? Are they faint or bold?
- Become aware of how your body is responding to the smell. Your body may go on sensory alert in anticipation of eating. Savor this anticipation.
- Are you starting to salivate?

STEP 3: FOOD ENTERS YOUR MOUTH

- And now, slowly put the raisin in your mouth. Don't bite it just yet.
- And as you are placing the raisin in your mouth, notice how your hand, arm, and mouth know precisely how to do this.

- Become aware of the sensations of having the raisin in your mouth. Explore the feelings generated in your mouth.
- And when you are ready, with awareness, slowly bite into the raisin. As your teeth gently sink into it, notice the taste as it releases.
- Notice the sensations as your teeth enter the raisin. Does it feel smooth or crunchy or something else?
- Ask yourself, what does the raisin taste like? How does it compare to other foods you have tasted before?
- Let the raisin warm up by spending some time in your mouth. Are there any changes in flavor?

Step 4: Chewing

- Breathe in and out through your nose as you taste.
- And when you are ready, slowly start chewing the raisin. Chew ten or more times to mix the flavors and textures and bring the odors to your nose.
- At this point, you may want to close your eyes so you can focus just on the tasting.
- When you are ready, roll the raisin around in your mouth. Let it hit all the taste buds on your tongue, mouth, and the roof of the mouth.
- On the first chew or two, if you feel comfortable, draw air through the raisin by pursing your lips and sucking in air as if through a straw. Suck in air for about 3

seconds. Then close your mouth and breathe out through your nose. Notice any flavors and aromas.
- Let your taste buds speak to you. Try to hold back from translating experience into words for a while until you have captured the flavor.
- Hold the raisin in your mouth long enough to register an impression. You will be confronted by a lot of different sensations. Now try to put your impressions into words. Concentrate on one thing at a time.
- Try to distinguish all of the different tastes: sweet, bitter, sour, salty, fat, and savory.
- Does your mouth feel like puckering? Does it feel tingly or dry? Do you detect any acidy or bitter flavors?
- Become aware of how the sensation of the raisin develops after the first impression.
- Notice if the taste changes and deepens, or whether it becomes weaker or flatter, or whether it sweetens and softens, or hardens.
- Become aware of the texture of the raisin in your mouth. Is it harsh? Oily? Fizzy? Smooth? Rough? Buttery? Silky? Watery? Creamy? Thick? Thin?
- Does the raisin have a rich, interesting, satisfyingly full taste?
- Is the flavor complex or simple?
- Is the flavor balanced? Does any one flavor overwhelm any of the others?

- Are there any missing flavors that you were expecting to taste?
- Continue to taste as the raisin cools. Some characteristics reveal themselves most clearly in cooler food.

STEP 5: SWALLOWING

- See if you can detect the intention to swallow as it arises before you actually swallow the raisin.
- And when you are ready, swallow the raisin...as you are swallowing, follow the sensation of the raisin moving out of your mouth, down your throat, and into your stomach.

STEP 6: AFTERWARD

- Take some time to notice how you feel after eating the raisin.
- How long does the taste of the raisin stay in your mouth?
- Notice what you taste and feel in your mouth. Is it sweet? Acidy?
- Burning? Is it fading or strong? Is your mouth drying out?

- Wait a few moments so you can appreciate the aftertaste. Are there any lingering flavors or mouth feelings?
- Notice any feelings of satisfaction.
- If the taste experience was exceptionally good, try to anchor it in your mind so you can recall it later.
- Talk about the raisin with your friends. Talk about how it tastes and feels. Try to find words to express your experience. Use conversation to heighten anticipation from the next bite and to learn more about raisins generally.

Following the six steps in Joyful Eating, you will have extracted every bit of pleasure from one bite. You will have experienced far more pleasure from one bite than you would from eating a lot more.

The Four Steps for Using Joyful Eating

There are four steps to apply Joyful Eating in any situation:

1. Decide which foods you want to Eat Joyfully.
2. Decide on your portion size.
3. Eat Joyfully.
4. Stop eating on reaching your portion size.

Scenario: Dinner Out

Let's go through an example of how to eat joyfully when you go out to dinner.

Step 1: Decide which foods you want to Eat Joyfully.

After browsing the menu and thinking about what I want to eat, I decide to eat bread, potato, and dessert joyfully. These are the high-carb items I love and are the foods I need to be most careful about. I also have to worry about calories for dessert, but Joyful Eating small portions naturally limits calories.

A large steak can have a lot of calories because of all the fat. I often try to pick a smaller steak. If I am not worried about calories that day, maybe because I had a long cardio workout, I'll go ahead and order a large steak. I always eat steak joyfully because it just tastes so good that way. You can also divide the steak in half and put some in a doggy bag for later.

I can usually share my wife's potato and dessert. You may need to ask around the table to see if anyone wants to share. If nobody will share, you can get a whole order and just eat your portion. Take the rest home or just leave it.

These days, I make a conscious effort to eat spicier foods. Being from the great Pacific Northwest, I was raised to consider salt and pepper exotic spices. Now spicy dishes excite me because they are an opportunity for a new taste experience. Plus, spices are low in carbs, fat, and calories. They add variety and excitement to your diet for almost no cost. Many people already know the secret of spice, but I thought slow people like me might want to try spicier food.

STEP 2: DECIDE ON YOUR PORTION SIZE.

After deciding what to eat joyfully, it's time to consider how much I'll eat.

If the bread doesn't look truly excellent, I'll usually decide not to eat it. I'd rather spend my carb budget on dessert or have a little more potato. One test for good bread is how it smells. A rich, complex smell usually means a bread worth eating. If I did eat the bread, I would make sure my one bite was covered in real melted butter. Yum.

I'll have one big spoonful each of the potato and the dessert. I may choose to have two bites each on a good exercise day. This is actually a good part of the system because it encourages me to have good exercise days!

I love a fully loaded-potato. I add sour cream, chives, butter, salt, and pepper. Joyful Eating is perfect for eating potato because potato has a very subtle flavor.

Choosing a dessert takes some real thought, and that's part of the fun. A lot of desserts are just layers of sugar. As tempting as loads of sugar may sound, sugar-only desserts won't satisfy. Sugar is just one of our tastes. Combining other tastes into your meals, like bitter, sour, salty, and savory, enriches your taste experience.

Cheesecake with a strawberry topping is often my choice. I find the aroma of cheesecake uplifting. It has a smooth, creamy texture with a good mouth feel. Cheesecake is both sweet and sour, which gives it a complexity I like. Even a single bite of cheesecake can take a while to eat. If you add nuts to the crust or topping, you also have a pleasurable contrast in textures. The fat in cheesecake gives it a rich deep taste. The flavor of cream cheese is mild and forms a good backdrop for a sweet topping. The contrast between the sweet strawberry flavor and the mild, slightly sour cheesecake can be very pleasing. And because cheesecake has a lot of calories, eating just one bite keeps down the calorie count.

I think about all of these issues before I order. If I don't, I stand a good chance of overeating, and I can't afford the health risk. If you don't plan ahead, it won't work. The temptations are too great.

Step 3: Eat Joyfully.

I eat joyfully as each food is delivered, following the steps we discussed earlier. In this case, the bread wasn't very good, so I passed on it. The potato and dessert were excellent.

Step 4: Stop eating on reaching your portion size.

I served myself the foods I would eat joyfully to ensure I only ate as much as I planned to eat.

I shared my wife's potato. I cut off my wanted amount and brought it over to my plate. I had two big bites of the potato because I didn't have any bread.

I also shared my wife's dessert. I served myself one big bite of her chocolate cake. Following the recommendation of the Joyful Eating steps, we talked about our experience of the cake as we were eating, which helped bring out the best taste from the cake.

One bite can be enough.

37. Habit: Maximize Food Pleasure

You can maximize the amount of pleasure you experience in your life by bringing it under conscious control.

You can use certain tricks to get more pleasure from a meal. Here are a few you might find fun to try.

Save the Best for Last

What you experience last dramatically influences how you think of your entire meal. Make the last bite great, and you'll feel better about all of it.

Eat a Greater Number of Smaller Courses

Your appetite and your pleasure increase by eating smaller selections of high-quality food. You don't always need to eat large meals.

Control Expectations

Having high expectations sets you up for almost inevitable disappointment. Go into a meal with an open mind and low expectations. Aim to be pleasantly surprised instead of knowingly dissatisfied.

Space Out Experiences

Your brain adapts to experiences if you have them too close together. Separate out how often you have a taste experience, and you'll enjoy it more.

Be Grateful

Don't talk about how much better the experience could have been. Look for the good in the experience you had.

Forget What You Didn't Choose

Don't think about the attractive food options you didn't take. This only builds up regret. Focus on enjoying what you did order and forget what you didn't choose.

Minimize Choices

Having lots of different choices builds up confusion and regret. If you order from a small set of excellent options, you'll be happier with your choice.

You Don't Always have to Try New Things

If you plan your meals for the next couple of weeks, you may be tempted to choose a lot of different meals because you think you will get bored if you have the same dishes every week. Surprisingly, this isn't true.

You won't get as bored as you think. If you like something, as long as you don't have it all the time, you'll like it the next time you eat it too.

If, for example, popcorn is a snack you love, you'll still enjoy it every day.

Eat the First Bite of Any Dish Joyfully

Eat the first bite of every dish joyfully. You'll increase your sensory stimulation and get the most satisfaction from all your meals by following this rule.

Keep Good Company

Eat with people who appreciate food and are willing to talk about the good points. It helps you appreciate food too.

Share Food in a Group

If you are in a group, a perfect Joyful Eating practice is to order food as a group and share it. Pass your bread plate around the table and have people put different foods on it. Everyone will get a **small** portion of a lot of different tastes. And everyone will have a chance to taste something truly excellent.

This trick works exceptionally well for desserts. A full dessert, though very tempting, will usually be a lot more calories than expected. As a group, order a few desserts and share them. Then each person can eat one or two perfect delicious bites.

I've noticed comfort with food sharing is highly cultural. My Chinese friends are at first bewildered by the American practice of eating individual meals, even at a Chinese restaurant! I used to be one of these people.

You may need to be brave and overturn custom by suggesting that your table share food. Not everyone will want to share, but a lot of people might. The other people will soon see how much fun you are having and throw their food into the mix.

Take Flavor Vacations

Not eating a flavor for a while revitalizes your ability to taste it. So take a 2-week vacation from sweet, salty, sour, or bitter flavors from time to time. Parting is such sweet sorrow, but the makeup tasting is excellent.

Smell What You Love

Your sense of smell deteriorates with age. You can fight back by taking a whiff of your favorite smell every day for a few months. This forces your body to create new scent receptors.

Search Out New Experiences

Look for interesting, rich, and complex foods. Look for new and different tastes. Look for fresh, colorful foods. Look for spicy foods. Look for subtle and simple foods. Food is an adventure, and you are an explorer. Go forth and eat well.

This doesn't contradict the idea that *You Don't Always have to Try New Things*. Both principles work if you use them well.

Plan Your Journey

The first time you experience a food may be the strongest experience you will have with it.

To re-create the first-time experience, you may want to leave time between eating the same kind of food. "Absence makes the heart grow fonder" applies to food as well. If, for example, you have dozens of strawberries every day, it may be challenging to find joy in each new strawberry. If you wait a week between strawberry tastings, you give your body a chance to forget about strawberries. Then the next strawberry will be a bolder experience.

If you plan your entire diet with this in mind, you can keep yourself at a continual peak of the eating experience. Certainly, there is also great delight in coming to know something completely. So mix it up. Keep your mind and taste buds off balance by combining short periods of new flavors with longer periods focused on a single family of flavors.

Think of your eating life as a journey. The key to a lifetime of eating pleasure is to avoid most of the ruts in the road and continually travel to new places while still managing to visit and stay with old friends along the way. You must consciously manage your journey; otherwise, you'll build up a series of habits and fears that will lock you into one boring path.

Planning your journey applies at many different points in time. You may pick different contrasting dishes within a meal. You may select different restaurant styles daily, weekly, or monthly. You may concentrate on wine from a particular region for a month. You may try cooking from different cuisines at home. You may fast for a day. You may go out to eat with different groups of friends. The possibilities are infinite.

38. Habit: Start with Soup or Salad

Have a salad or cup of soup to take the edge off of your hunger.

The idea behind this habit is to fill up on tasty, high-volume, low-calorie food so you can enjoy smaller portions of great-tasting main dishes while still feeling full.

When you start a meal with a large portion of a food with a lot of bulk and few calories, like soup or salad, it makes you feel full, so you end up eating less for the rest of your meal.

Researchers have found that people who ate a big salad before eating the main course ate fewer calories overall than those who didn't have a salad.

One study found that eating a large low-calorie salad reduced the overall calories for the entire meal by 107 calories. Eating a large high-calorie salad had the opposite result: the total calories for the entire meal increased by 145 calories.

This habit is surprisingly effective and easy. I use it almost every day. Both broth-based soup and salad taste wonderful, so you aren't losing any quality from your meal. And by eating the salad, you feel full enough that you can eat a smaller portion of a food you really love and still feel full. It's a win-win.

39. Habit: Ask for a Doggy Bag Immediately

Decide how much you are going to eat before taking the first bite. Put the rest in a to-go container *before* you start eating.

Restaurant portions are about twice the size they were in the past. A full restaurant meal may supply most of your daily calories. **You can't change how much food a restaurant serves you, but you can change how much you eat.**

As you order, **immediately** ask your server for a to-go container. Don't wait. Do it now.

When your food arrives, **immediately** put your predetermined portion into the to-go container as soon as it is brought to your table. Don't wait. Do it now.

Don't fool yourself that you'll stop eating later. You probably won't. Once you start eating the food will taste so good you simply won't stop.

By following this habit, you are both cutting down on how much you are eating and you also have an excellent meal for the next day. Think of it as getting two meals for the price of one with the added bonus of staying on your diet!

40. Habit: Split Meals with a Friend

Buy one meal and split it with a friend.

Gigantic restaurant meals make it realistic to buy one meal and split it between two people. If you need a little extra food, then buy an appetizer or two. Most restaurants will give you an extra plate if you ask nicely.

Remember to leave a full tip for your server. They are still doing all the work. Leaving a tip based on the price of one meal wouldn't be fair.

41. Habit: Use Meal Replacements

> Meal replacements are convenient, portion-controlled, relatively low-calorie meals that fill you up.

A meal replacement is a drink or bar you eat instead of a meal. Your breakfast, for example, would be a meal replacement bar or shake instead of your normal cereal and toast or bacon and eggs.

Nobody was more skeptical about using meal replacements than I was. I was sure they were a scam created by food manufacturers to extract yet more money out of consumers.

However, when I looked into the research, there was a lot of evidence showing meal replacements work, even over many years of use. Using meal replacement, people are able to stay on their diets, lose up to 8% of their body weight, and keep the weight off.

Why do meal replacements seem to work so well?

- **It's easy so you can do it every day.** Eating a bar or fixing a shake is easy so people can stick to it over the long term. It's not a habit you easily get tired of.
- **It protects you from slip-ups by reducing the number of decisions you have to make.** When fixing your own meals, there is always the chance of overeating. Using a meal replacement guarantees you a fixed meal size and number of calories. It's an easy form of portion control.
- **You feel full.** Meal replacements are formulated to help you feel full after eating them. This reduces your need to snack which reduces your total number of calories.

In short, meal replacements work because of portion control. You are eating a fixed-size, relatively low-calorie meal that fills you up.

A breakfast, for example, may have three times the calories of a meal replacement. By eating meal replacements you are controlling your portions.

Usually, people replace only one meal a day, but it has been shown to be safe and effective to replace two daily meals. Just make sure you eat healthy snacks and dinner during the rest of the day.

Which meal replacement should you use?

Through experiment and research, I have created my own meal replacement shake, but if you look around you'll find plenty to choose from. There are all different kinds on the market for all different needs and ways of eating.

Experiment with different products to see which you like best. Do you prefer a bar or a shake? What mix of protein, carbs, and other nutrients are you looking for? Does it fill you up? What flavors do you like? How much does it cost?

There are so many products it may take a bit of research to find which one works for you. But if you have trouble with portion control, the meal replacement habit may be an excellent choice for you.

42. Habit: Use Pre-Prepared Meals

> You can control your portion sizes using pre-prepared meals while still eating quality food.

The art of portion control is figuring out ways to make yourself eat only the amount of food you intend.

For many of the same reasons we discussed in the *Use Meal Replacements* habit, you might find pre-prepared meals an excellent habit for enforcing portion control.

Pre-prepared meals are ready-to-eat or near-ready-to-eat, are quick and easy to make, and have a known calorie count for a known portion size. That's a significant advantage over eating out or fixing your own meals.

One of the under-appreciated benefits of using pre-packaged foods is they **teach you what proper portion sizes look like.** We have become so used to large portion sizes we don't know what a proper-sized piece of chicken or serving of pasta looks like anymore.

What are some of your pre-prepared meal options?

- **Meal Kits.** There are so many meal kit options these days. A meal kit combines the benefits of a meal preparation service and frozen dinners. They provide a menu of meals to choose from, do all the shopping, and then perform all or some of the meal preparation steps. You "cook" the meals in your home. The advantage is that you get a wide variety of fresh food with known portion sizes. The disadvantage is that they can be expensive.
- **Healthy Frozen Dinners.** Frozen dinners were horrible at one time. That's not as true anymore. Many good-quality, low-calorie frozen dinners are available now.
- **Prepackaged Dinners.** Look in the refrigerator section of your store for complete prepackaged ready-to-cook meals for your family. New products are coming onto the market all the time.
- **Personal Chef Service.** Meal preparation services have become a lot more popular lately. They can include personalized meal planning, grocery shopping, and the preparation of dinners. They do all the

cooking for you. There is a wide variety of different options, depending on your budget and preferences. You can pick up pre-prepared meals each day, or you can take home a bunch of meals for later. Compared to frozen or pre-packaged dinners, the advantage of using a meal preparation service is that the food should be fresher, higher quality, more nutritious, and better tasting.
- **Full-Time Personal Chef.** If you have the resources, a personal chef is a good hire. Your expert cook can make a wide variety of the foods you like while keeping your calorie budget in mind.

You don't always have to make your own meals or always eat pre-prepared meals. You may want to cook on the weekends when you have time and use pre-prepared meals on the weekdays when time is short. Cook when and if you want.

Overall the meal is healthy and portion-controlled, and there's minimal opportunity for slipping up—all fine attributes of a great habit.

43. Habit: Use Smaller Plates and Bowls

> **Your plate size determines how much you will eat. Eat from smaller dinnerware, and you'll naturally control your portion sizes.**

We unconsciously eat more from larger packages. Plates have become much larger in recent years. That's a weight-gaining combination if ever there was one.

A good counter-move is to right-size all your plates, bowls, glasses, cups, and spoons so that they fit your portion sizes. You may think this habit is a bit silly, but it's **amazingly effective**.

Think about how you serve food. If you are filling a big plate from a big serving bowl, you will likely fill the entire plate with food. Your plate size then determines how much you will eat.

Simply by using smaller dishes, you reduce the amount of food you serve yourself without even trying (or thinking about it).

One of my most successful strategies ever was **replacing a standard soup bowl** with a much smaller dessert bowl. Now I use a dessert bowl that is already the correct portion size for the amount of dessert I should eat—using a dessert bowl for dessert, what a radical idea!

Dessert bowls always looked small to me. But they aren't. Carefully measure how much ice cream you put in a soup bowl. It could easily be over 1,000 calories. Do the same for a dessert bowl, the calories will be much more reasonable.

I also bought smaller plates. A big plate just demands to be filled up. The smaller plate is more like the portion size I should be eating, so it is much easier to eat the right amount of food.

Where do you find smaller dishes and utensils? It's not easy. You have to look around. Dishes were smaller in the past, so you can often find old sets of smaller dishes at garage sales. I hope in the future; some manufacturers will step up and make attractive portion-controlled dishes.

I try never to rely on my ability to stop eating. I use every habit I can to ensure I always eat the right amount of food, so it's impossible for me to eat more than I should.

44. Habit: Break Up Food into Smaller Packages

Smaller packages ensure the proper serving size and give you a chance to stop eating after each serving.

After grocery shopping, repackage your food into the appropriate serving sizes. This habit helps ensure you won't eat too much.

Let's say you have cookies. How many cookies do you want to eat at one time? Let's say three. Now take the cookies out of the box and put three cookies each into separate plastic bags.

Breaking up the larger container into individual serving sizes accomplishes two goals:

- **You don't have to think about the proper serving size.** It's built into your packaging. This means you won't accidentally overeat because the portion sizes will be correct.
- **You give yourself a chance to stop eating after each serving.** When food is in a large package, there is no natural stopping point, so you just keep eating. With smaller packages, you get a natural place to stop and think to yourself that you have had enough.

When I get home from shopping, I break out the zip-lock bags and the scale, and I repackage food into its proper portion sizes. It's not something I look forward to, but I find if I don't do it, I will eat too much.

The first time you measure and repackage your food, you may be shocked at how much you have been eating. I repackage the hamburger into 1/4 pound patties for my wife and 1/2 pound patties for me. A 1/4 pound is a lot smaller than I remember.

I was stunned by how much spaghetti I ate before I started using pre-packaged quantities. A serving of spaghetti, for the kind I buy, is 2 ounces for 190 calories. The quantity I used to eat was easily 5 times that!

I have found several ways of making the packaging job easier:

- **Use a good electric scale.** It makes measuring a lot faster.

- **Buy a lot of zip-locked baggies.** You need something to put those smaller portions into.
- **Buy right-sized pre-packaged food portions from the start.** Cheese, for example, comes packaged in slices. Even though the slices are more expensive, it's worth it. Cookies and crackers are now sold in one-hundred-calorie serving sizes. Carrots are now sold in single-serving sizes. It's a trend I expect will continue.
- **Don't repackage vegetables.** You want to eat more of them.
- **Some foods aren't easily repackageable.** Nuts, for example, are difficult to repackage because there are so many of them, and the serving size is so small. I know I should only eat ten almonds at a time, so I just take ten from the jar. I'll consider not buying something if it's hard to repackage. Other foods are just hard, like salad dressing. It's not practical to repackage salad dressing, yet it has a lot of calories in a small amount, so I make sure I am careful when measuring out a serving.
- **Be creative.** You can usually overcome any problems with a little thought and a firm understanding of the reason for repackaging food. The idea is to make it hard for you to slip up and eat more than you should. Just apply the no slip-up idea whenever you can.

Repackaging is a habit you should revisit when you notice you are gaining weight. Over time it's so easy for portion sizes to creep up. Repackaging food into smaller portion sizes is a habit that prevents your portion sizes from slowly creeping up over time.

45. Habit: Follow The Goody Rules

Reduce the goodies to control your weight.

The Goody Rules are strategies for reducing the pressure goodies exert on your brain to eat them. When goodies are around, and you know they're around, your brain targets them like a laser pointer.

To control your weight, you need to change your environment to reduce the goody threat. Here are a few strategies for countering the power of the goody:

Put Goodies in Opaque Containers

Simply using a container you can't see into helps stop unintentional eating. One study found that people ate many fewer chocolates from an opaque bowl, meaning they couldn't see the contents of the bowl. Out of sight, out of mind.

Place Goodies Far Away

The closer food is to you, the more food you will eat. So put the goodies out of the way.

Simply by placing food out of reach, you will reduce the amount you eat from mountain to molehill. If you didn't have a remote control, how often would you change channels? The same habit works for food.

The harder something is to do, the less you will do it, and placing food far away gives you the natural pause you need to rethink your urge to snack.

It's similar to the idea of repackaging foods into correct portion sizes instead of eating from a large container.

The **distance you must travel** to eat your goody gives you time to rethink and stop what you are doing.

This habit applies in every area you can think of: home, work, school, and in your car. Don't leave convenient jars of snacks in your office, on a counter, or on your desk. Keep candy-filled vending machines far away.

Treat bad foods like vampires—never invite them in.

Go Out for Goodies

If your environment contains goodies, you will hunt them down and eat them.

The best way to put yourself in a position to succeed is to simply not have goodies in the house. If you want a treat, go out and get it.

Pack up the family, zoom off and get a scoop of ice cream. The mere fact that you have to make a special effort prevents the majority of treat trips.

How extreme do you need to be in this habit? As always, you have to decide for yourself and for your family.

I decided I had to be extreme. I found myself eating too many ice cream bars (even low-calorie ones) when they were around, so I simply got rid of them. If I really want one, I can go down to the store. If you look in our house, there aren't any goodies.

Well, that's not completely true. I keep around bars of high-quality dark chocolate. Dark chocolate is a wonderful dessert because I feel completely satisfied Joyfully Eating two squares. And get this…two squares of delicious dark chocolate only have 100 calories! And for some reason, I don't pig out on the dark chocolate, which means I can keep it in the house without worrying I'll make an occasional slip-up.

Use Tall Thin Drinking Glasses

People naturally pour up to 32% more of a drink into shorter and wider containers. That's a lot of extra calories! You can help prevent yourself from drinking too much simply by buying different-shaped glasses. How's that for creating a healthy habit!

46. Habit: Don't Eat from a Container

Take the amount of food you want to eat out of its container and put it in a separate dish, especially for binge foods like potato chips and ice cream.

When you eat potato chips out of the bag, how often do you keep eating until you reach the bottom?

Portion control is almost impossible when eating out of a container. Avoid the temptation entirely by not eating out of containers in the first place.

Instead, serve yourself exactly how much you think you should eat into a separate appropriately sized dish and eat out of that dish, not the container.

This one is very difficult for me. After dinner, I place the leftovers in a plastic container. The next day when I am hungry, the most natural thing in the world is to eat directly out of the container. Why dirty another dish? I always have to remember to take just my portion size out or I'll eat too much almost every time.

47. Habit: Don't Bring Serving Dishes to the Table

Fill your plate with as much food as you are going to eat for the entire meal *before* sitting down to eat at the table.

At family-style meals, it's traditional to bring big heaping serving dishes filled with food to the table. Individuals then serve themselves directly out of the huge serving dishes using gigantic serving spoons. Can you guess why this style of eating may be bad for your waistline?

- The serving dishes and utensils are large, so chances are you'll spoon more food than you should onto your plate.

- The serving dishes tease you by staying on the table while you are eating. Your chances of having seconds and even thirds go way up.
- Eating with friends and family encourages you to linger over the meal, which increases your chances of eating more.

Who knew the family dinner table was such a minefield? To avoid temptation, serve each person's plate with their appropriate amount of food and put the rest of the food out of reach. To be really safe, put all the leftover food away before you eat.

48. Habit: Trick Yourself into Eating More Healthy Food

You can reverse many of the "do not" suggestions in previous habits to trick yourself into eating more healthy foods instead of just figuring out how to avoid bad foods.

Let's say you, for example, want to eat more baby carrots because they are filling and healthy. What do you do?

Put the carrots into a large clear container and put this close while working. You can also set the carrots within easy reach in the refrigerator. You can use the same idea with salads, vegetable plates, and anything else you want people to eat more of.

I am constantly amazed at the difference this approach makes. If I hide carrots in the refrigerator's vegetable drawer, I won't think about them when a snack attack hits. But if they're plain view, I'll eat them first instead of settling for a worse choice.

We keep hard-boiled eggs in our refrigerator as a filling snack. Eggs are healthy, fixed-sized, and have a natural stopping point to discourage overeating.

A funny thing happens, though. When only a few eggs are left in the bowl, we stop eating them. When more eggs are in the bowl, we eat more of them.

So when the egg bowl goes low, I ensure to fill it up again. We'd probably switch to a less healthy snack if we didn't. I've noticed the same situation happens with apples too.

If you want your family to eat more fruit, have a big fruit basket displayed proudly on a kitchen counter next to the refrigerator.

Don't have junk food in the house. It has been found that even when healthier foods are available, people will still eat junk food if it is around. **If you only have good food around, then that's all you can eat.**

With a bit of thought and creativity, I am sure you can come up with many ideas that will work for you and your family.

49. Habit: Eat Meals at Home with Your Family

Your home environment will help protect you from overeating.

People eat away from home more than ever these days. The temptation of eating at a restaurant combined with the huge portion sizes is a definite threat to your diet.

Staying on a diet while eating out all the time is like running with a hundred-pound rock on your back. You can probably do it, but it's really hard.

Try eating at home more often. If you've adopted the habits we've been talking about, your home environment will help protect you from overeating.

At home, you can't cheat because you've only purchased the foods you purposefully decided to eat.

50. Habit: Learn to Cook

Until you can answer the "what's to eat" question, you are always vulnerable to slipping up and eating the wrong foods.

Is this you and your family?

Cook? Me? You must be kidding. I can't even boil water! We eat out a lot. Mostly pizza and fast food. There are so many choices, and the kids don't make a fuss. But, we keep sandwich fixings' around and stuff you can pop in the micro too. —Anonymous

As late as the 1960s, it may not have been possible to feed a family without cooking. The environment has changed. Now a family can eat out every day. Fast food is cheap, kids love it, and you'll never get bored because of the vast variety of available fast food restaurants.

The problem is fast food is associated with poor nutrition and obesity. Yes, I know you can make better choices, but most of the time, people don't.

What's the easiest thing to do when you don't have a plan for a meal? Go out. Restaurant portions are enormous, and it is very tempting to eat something you shouldn't.

If you choose not to eat out, then the chances are you will go home and graze, eating lots of different things without much control over the quantity or quality of the food. A bag of chips may seem like the perfect answer when you are hungry.

How can you answer the "what's to eat" question? We've already discussed a few possibilities: meal replacements and pre-prepared foods. Another answer is: **learn how to cook.**

A family that eats together eats better, according to a recent study in the *Archives of Family Medicine.* The study showed children who report frequent family dinners have healthier diets than their peers who don't.

There are a lot of places to learn how to cook. Hopefully, someone in your family is a good cook and is willing to teach you. Consider books, magazines, schools, city parks & recreation departments, community colleges, gourmet food stores, and formal cooking schools. Even some health plans, like Kaiser Permanente, offer virtual and in-person cooking classes. And don't forget all the cooking shows on TV! There are plenty of sources to learn how to cook, so give it a try.

Try involving your children in the meal-making process from a young age. When they are preschoolers, teach them how to set the table. Take them grocery shopping and let them pick some treats, fruits, and vegetables. Have a family night and let the kids cook some of the meal. Giving children more and more supervised responsibility over time helps them become capable and better able to make healthy decisions as they grow older.

The sheer joy of cooking is one of life's gifts that many in the modern world have lost touch with. The ritual of preparing food and eating together is as ancient as humanity, and it can reconnect us in a deep and satisfying way, if we let it.

51. Habit: Structure Your Meal Plans

Plan exactly what you're going to eat and why. People using meal plans lost 50% more weight than people not using meal plans and kept the weight off better over time.

A meal plan is an exact plan of what to eat every day, combined with a shopping list of which foods you need to buy to cook all the planned meals. Your meal plan tells you exactly which foods to buy, how much to buy, what meals you will make, and when you will eat them.

Why is using a food plan such a strong habit for losing weight and staying on your diet?

- Following your chosen diet becomes much simpler because **you've reduced the number of decisions** you have to make. Eating outside your meal plan won't be easy because that's the only food you'll have easily available.
- Your portions will be **correctly sized** because you planned them to be the right size. There's no guessing involved. And by having known portion sizes, you are also learning better calorie estimation skills. This also helps to stop overeating.
- You will eat **better quality food.** You can pick better recipes that are more nutritious, so you end up eating better.
- You will **snack less and eat more regularly.** Eating breakfast, lunch, and dinner decreases the temptation to snack or skip meals.

The problem is meal planning can be hard because it, well, requires planning! It's always easier not to plan.

How might you go about creating a meal plan?

- **Realize that this isn't easy.** Meal planning is a skill you develop with practice.
- **Pick a planning day.** When are you going to plan your meals? Sunday is a common day, but it can be any convenient day. A typical meal plan lasts a week because food can normally stay fresh for that long, but you can use any time period that works for you.

- **Who will do the planning?** Consider rotating the task if someone doesn't take the job on permanently. Remember to involve kids in the process, so they can learn how to plan meals for when they grow up.
- **Pick a shopping day.** When will you go shopping? Sunday is a typical shopping day, but you can pick any day. You can also make several shorter weekly trips to pick up fresh foods like fruits and vegetables and anything else you might have forgotten.
- **Know your way of eating.** What type of diet will your family eat? What's the target calorie budget for each person? Do any of your family members have special dietary needs? If so, how will you accommodate them?
- **Have a backup plan if you're busy.** What happens when life gets in the way, and you didn't do the meal planning or didn't go shopping yet? Have a backup plan so your family can still eat a healthy meal.
- **Find sources of meal plans.** Meal planning is a vast topic. You can find lots of advice in cookbooks at your local library or online. Ask your family and friends too. Many people love to cook and are full of great ideas. There are also many meal planning services available on the Internet. And you may already have a massive batch of cookbooks. Always be on the lookout for new sources of meal ideas.
- **Recycle meal plans.** Find out what your family likes and keep making it. People don't get bored with meals

when served relatively far apart. Include new meals in your plans, but don't think you always have to be inventive. This puts too much stress on you; the more stress you feel, the less likely you are to plan meals. Old favorites are old favorites for a reason: people like them.
- **Use seasonal meal plans.** Vegetables and fruits are usually much cheaper and better tasting when they come into season.

Your risk of overeating is almost non-existent if you only buy what you plan on eating.

52. Habit: Pump Up the Volume–Feeling Full from Fewer Calories

---

To feel fuller, eat foods with the same weight and fewer calories.

There's a weight control habit most people haven't heard of called *Volumetrics*. Dr. Barbara Rolls, a well-respected food-nutrition researcher at Pennsylvania State University, created Volumetrics.

She found the "eat less" part of "eat less and exercise more" isn't true. You can eat less and gain a ton of weight. You can also eat a lot more and still lose weight.

This amazingly counterintuitive finding hinges on Dr. Rolls' research showing that people eat about the same weight of food each day, regardless of the food's calorie content. Your body doesn't seem to pay attention to the number of calories in food when deciding whether you are full. This finding has significant implications for your weight.

The idea behind *Volumetrics* is that if you eat food with the same weight and fewer calories, you can eat more and weigh less. The relationship between what a food weighs and the number of calories it has is called its **energy density.**

Cookies are an excellent example of a high-energy-dense food. Cookies have a lot of calories in a little package because they are made from a lot of fat and sugar. Fat has the most energy, at nine calories per gram. If your food is high in fat, it is also high in calories.

Celery is an excellent example of a low-energy-dense food because it has low calories for its weight. Celery has a lot of water and fiber at almost no calories.

The difference between raisins and grapes is an excellent example of how eating a low-calorie-dense food can help you feel full for fewer calories. You may think you feel full faster on higher-calorie food, but unfortunately, that's not how it works.

Let's say you are eating a small, high-calorie food like raisins. You'll eat a lot of raisins before you start feeling full because each raisin is small. And because each raisin is high in calories, you eat a lot more calories than you probably intend. One-quarter cup of raisins is 100 calories. One and two-thirds cups of whole grapes is 100 calories.

For the same 100 calories, which will fill you more: 1⁄4 cup of raisins or 1 2⁄3 cup of grapes? The grapes! Grapes are a lower energy-dense food than raisins. The grapes take up more space for the same number of calories. Grapes are a good deal. You get to eat more grapes than raisins and feel fuller.

So the big idea of Volumetrics is to **lower the energy density** of the food you eat. This allows you to eat a lot more food for the same calories, just like you can eat more grapes than raisins for the same calories.

You can lower the energy density of a typical dish like a casserole by **adding more vegetables** and **using less cheese** and low-fat milk. Using less cheese and reduced-fat milk means fewer calories because there is less fat. Vegetables are high in fiber and water while low in calories. The overall result is a dish with the **same weight but fewer calories,** and you'll still feel full!

The same idea can be applied to hamburgers. Add vegetables to your hamburger, and you lower its calorie density, yet it will still be filling and taste just as good. Adding fruits and vegetables to most dishes reduces the number of calories in the dish while at the same time keeping you feeling full.

You may be asking, why can't you just drink water? Your stomach knows the difference between food and water. You have to eat real food to feel full. But you can use broth because it combines a lot of liquid and real food. This is why soup is so filling.

Volumetrics works.

One study found that increasing the amount of fruits and vegetables in your diet means you eat **400 fewer calories daily.**

And at the same time, you don't feel hungry. It's not hard to understand why. It's the volume of food that makes you feel full.

You can eat a large volume of water and fiber from fruits and vegetables without eating a lot of calories. The same volume of fatty foods would be an enormous number of calories.

A series of Swedish studies found that **simply adding carrots, spinach, and other high-fiber vegetables to your meals** can significantly lengthen the time it takes you to feel hungry again.

Volumetrics isn't a fad diet. It's a well-researched idea. The trick is getting fewer calories for the same weight of food.

53. Habit: Use a Shopping List

> **A shopping list prompts you to plan meals, prevents you from buying foods you don't need, and encourages you to eat the portions and types of foods you desire.**

Here's how I used to shop. I had no regular shopping day. When I was out of enough stuff, it was time to go shopping. I hate shopping, so delaying until the last possible minute was the standard plan. I could go days without vegetables or other good foods because it wasn't time to shop yet. Meals were made from whatever I could find or pick up on the way home.

When it was finally time to shop, I had no plan. I just went to the store and bought stuff that looked good. I didn't know how to cook, so I had no idea about making meals. I had no meal plan, so a balanced diet hung on whatever moved me as I stalked the aisles. What did I pick to eat? Lots of spaghetti. Ice cream, of course. Cereal. Not many fruits or vegetables.

Oh, the bad old days! What do the good new days look like? Make a meal plan, as we discussed in the Structure Your Meal Plans habit, of what you will eat each week. Part of a meal plan is a shopping list of exactly which groceries you plan to buy. A lot of people stumble on the creating the shopping list step because it's hard. Fortunately, there's a secret to painless shopping list maintenance.

Keep a Running Shopping List

The secret to easy, pain-free shopping list creation is to **update your list as you run out of an item.** Keep a pad of paper in the kitchen. As soon as you run low on something, turn around and write it down on your shopping list. With this habit, you'll never run out of what you need.

For an even smoother shopping experience, divide your shopping list into different sections based on where you need to go shopping for an item. For example, if you run out of dog food, write it under the pet store section. If you run out of a spice, write it under a section for your spice store. And so on for all your items. Organizing your shopping trip is much simpler using this approach.

Shopping becomes less stressful because you already know most of what you need. You'll add more items when creating your meal plan, but most of what you'll need will already be written down.

You won't wander around the store wondering if you need this or that. You'll know exactly what you need to buy and be confident of having what you need. Otherwise, you'll buy food you don't need and more food than you need, both of which encourage you to overeat.

Use a Generated Shopping List

If you are using an online meal planning service like *Eat This Much*, it will not only generate personalized meal plans for you, it will generate a shopping list for you. That's as easy as it gets!

The List Should Specify Quantities

Your shopping list must specify precisely how much of each item you need. For example, don't just write down spaghetti on your shopping list; write down how many packages or ounces of spaghetti you should buy.

Why is this so important? If you don't buy the exact quantity you need, you will be tempted by store signs suggesting how many you should buy.

Only Buy What's on the List

This is a hard one: **buy only the amount of each item you specify on your shopping list and no more.**

Research has shown a sign that says, "Soup, no limit per person," will cause you to buy more, even if there isn't a special on the soup. Just putting a number in the price tag, like saying 3 for 2 dollars, makes you think about buying three items instead of the one item you needed.

Stores have many of these tricks. Putting items at the end of an aisle or candy at the checkout line makes you more likely to buy them impulsively. These tricks are so subtle and silent that you won't even notice they are working on you.

That's why stores are such a significant danger zone. You will be tricked into buying foods you weren't planning to and don't need. The result is overeating.

Sticking exactly to your shopping list prevents all these problems from happening in the first place. If your list says you need so much of a food item, that's all you buy. You don't have to think about it. If there's a sale on candy bars and it's not on your list, you don't buy it. You don't have to think about it.

The list reduces the number of decisions you have to make. You created the list at your strongest. When you are in a store, you're at your weakest because all the tricks are working on you, and you are imagining what a deal you are getting or you imagine how good something will taste.

Why such a strict rule? Two reasons:

- **The more food you buy, the more you will eat.** So don't buy it. Disregarding your list encourages you to buy more food than you need.
- **You will probably buy foods you shouldn't eat.** You are at your strongest when you make your shopping list. You are being thoughtful about what you should be eating and why. Sticking to your shopping list prevents you from buying the wrong foods.

Just stick to your shopping list, and you'll be safe.

54. Habit: Use the Hunt and Gather Method of Shopping

Eliminate temptation by taking each item on your list and going directly to that item in the store.

There are two main shopping styles: visit every aisle, and hunt and gather.

In the **visit every aisle** approach, you go up and down every aisle no matter what is on your shopping list. The problem is that you buy stuff that's not on your list. You see a treat, imagine how good it will taste, and plop it in your cart. When shopping with kids, this happens a lot.

The other approach, the strategy I recommend, is to **hunt and gather.** With hunt and gather, you go directly to each item on your shopping list. This approach eliminates a lot of chances for temptation. If you are not shopping every aisle, you are far less likely to buy items you don't need. And once you remember the layout of your store, hunt and gather shopping is a lot speedier.

A complete shopping list is the key to hunt and gather shopping. We have already talked about meal planning and shopping list creation.

Without a list with everything you need, you'll fall back to visiting every aisle, which means you will buy stuff you don't need. One time we had three large bottles of ketchup because I kept thinking we needed more ketchup!

There's a third method of shopping—use a shopping service to do your shopping for you. The advantage of using a service is there's no way you'll buy stuff that's not on your shopping list!

55. Habit: Eat Calories, Don't Drink Them

Don't drink sugary sodas or juices. Soft drinks are our largest single source of daily calories, providing more than 7%.

SODA HAS A LOT OF CALORIES! Sorry for shouting, but for some reason, many people don't realize that all the soda they pound down throughout the day has a lot of calories. Just because soda is a liquid doesn't mean it's a free food.

Soft drinks are our largest single source of daily calories, providing more than 7% of them. The 7-Eleven Double Gulp holds 64 ounces of soda and comes in at **800 calories.**

It's not just sodas that are the problem. Fruit juices have become popular but are equally high in calories while providing little nutrition. Children who drank more than four glasses of fruit juice on the day of a study were more than twice as likely to be overweight or obese compared to children who did not drink these drinks.

Here are some potential alternatives to drinking sugary sodas and fruit juices:

- If you hate diet soda, go heavy on the ice when filling the glass. You'll save a lot of calories by fooling yourself into thinking you're drinking a full glass of soda.
- Adding some lemon to diet soda may make it taste better to you.
- In general, liquid calories are far more fattening than filling. Eat your fruit rather than drink fruit juice. You can enjoy an apple or orange for the calories in one box of apple juice. And whole foods fill you up better than liquids and are more nutritious.
- Try drinking water in the morning instead of fruit juice. Fruit juice has a ton of calories. If you want nutrition, then eat fruit instead.

Switching to diet soda will save you hundreds of calories a day. For every 20 ounces of regular soda, you're consuming 250 calories. Drink several sodas a day, and you can quickly down 1,000 calories. That is most of your daily calorie budget spent for nothing!

56. Habit: Snack Smart

Always have healthy snacks available for when you are hungry. Otherwise, you'll eat unhealthy snacks.

Snack time is danger time. You are the most likely to go off your diet when hunting and gathering food for a snack.

Here are a few ideas on how to deal with snacks:

- **Always have healthy snacks available for when you are hungry.** Try baby carrots, fruit, hard-boiled eggs, or some other food that makes sense. If you have good food, you can eat on demand; you'll make better food choices.

- When you get the urge to splurge on a snack instead of sitting down to the entire bag of chips, take the appropriate serving size and put it in a separate dish. This will probably be enough to satisfy your craving.
- **Pay attention to hidden calories.** When you grab a candy bar at the check-out counter and then a super-size dinner, you add many calories you might not notice.
- **Try fat-free microwave popcorn** sprinkled with some Cajun seasoning or a packet of sweetener. Use an oil-free microwave popper to save on fats.
- **Cut out fried foods.** Healthier choices are grilling, baking, roasting, broiling, or boiling. Or try something different like sous vide or air fry cooking.

You need to take steps now to ensure that you are prepared when a snack attack hits.

57. Habit: Eat More Fruits and Vegetables to Eat Less Fat and Sugar

Eat more fruits and vegetables for lower weight and better health.

Let's assume you think eating more fruits and vegetables, and less fat and sugar are important. What's the best way to eat more of the good stuff and less of the bad stuff?

Focus on What You Should Eat, Not What You Shouldn't Eat

Interestingly, it has been found more effective to focus on what you should eat rather than what you shouldn't eat.

Don't say, for example, eat less fat and sugar. Instead, concentrate on eating more fruits and vegetables. By eating more fruits and vegetables, you may naturally eat less fat and sugar. It's very similar to the idea we discussed earlier about being less inactive as the way to get kids to exercise more.

Sometimes the indirect way is best.

Kids Follow the Leader

It is more effective to get parents to eat more fruits and vegetables than to concentrate on getting children to eat healthily. The family follows the parents.

This makes sense, doesn't it? If you have an overweight child, just trying to make the child eat healthier doesn't seem to work. What kid won't eat a bag of chips if they see their mother or father doing so?

What seems to work is parents leading by example, showing their children how and what to eat. Parents have a lot of power in this area, far more than they realize.

The problem is that parents are often overweight, too, so their family environment helps keep everyone overweight instead of on their diet. Ideally, parents need to educate themselves about the benefits of fruits and vegetables in their diet, then educate their children, and then translate what they have learned into changes in the food they buy and cook.

Why Eat Fruits and Vegetables?

You might think everyone just knows to eat more fruits and vegetables.

We hear through public service announcements that we should do so, but we have all learned how to tune out advertisements by now.

Before researching this habit, I admit I didn't know why I should eat more fruits and vegetables either. There are many reasons: they can help you lose weight and protect against heart disease, cancer, stroke, and numerous other health problems. Now I try to put more fruits and vegetables in my diet.

The recommendation is we should eat five servings of fruits and vegetables every day, but they never say how much is in a serving! I eventually tracked down this information. A serving size may not be not as much as you think:

- One medium fruit (apple, orange, banana, pear)
- 1/2 cup cut-up fruit
- 1/2 cup raw or cooked vegetables
- 1/4 cup dried fruit (raisins, apricots, mango)
- 1 cup raw, leafy vegetables
- 1/2 cup cooked or canned peas or beans
- 3/4 cup (6 ounces) 100% fruit or vegetable juice

This is a pretty low requirement. There are so many obvious health and weight benefits to eating more fruits and vegetables that you may want to consider adding more to your diet.

58. Habit: Drive Away from Temptation

Change your driving route if it puts you in temptation's way.

Every day for years, when going to work, I drove by a donut shop with the best donuts I've ever tasted. These were awesome donuts. And because I am an early-to-rise person, they were always hot and fresh. I can still taste them, though I haven't had a donut for many years.

I didn't have a donut every day, as you might expect. I would have a donut once a week. But as we have seen, little slip-ups add up, which was enough for me to gain weight.

Part of my environment was a risk to me. Good willpower got me a long way, but I needed to be extreme and put myself in the best position to succeed. So I changed my route. I drove a different way to work so I wouldn't drive by the donut shop anymore. Out of sight, out of mind.

59. Habit: Don't Eat in Your Car

How extreme do you need to be? Maybe you need to ban eating in your car.

It's so easy to overeat in a car. With ubiquitous drive-thru fast-food restaurants, it's easy to load up on food without even getting out of your car. For many people, eating in their car is simply too dangerous. Perhaps you should consider making it a rule that you just won't eat in a car.

60. Habit: Pack Your Own Food

Pack good food for the road rather than buy fast food on the run.

A lot of people live on the road. Salespeople, parents, commuters, and vacationers are just some of the groups who spend a lot of time in their cars. When the hunger drive hits, the next stop is usually the drive-through window of one of our many fine fast-food restaurants, and then it's back on the road again.

And while it's possible to eat healthy at a fast food restaurant, the chances are very much against it. So if you spend a lot of time in your car, how can you put yourself in the best position to control your weight?

Buy a small cooler and pack your food to take along with you. You can pack healthy snacks and tasty meals. It can be even more convenient than fast food because you don't have to stop traveling to eat.

And there are advantages to packing your food other than staying on your diet. You'll save money. You can reload food supplies from any grocery store. And you can decide to either eat in your car or stop and picnic at any beautiful spot along the way. Fast food restaurants aren't known for their beautiful locations. Picnicking in a lovely park or beside a river transforms any meal into a feast.

Packing a healthy lunch makes it easier to stay on your diet.

Packing lunch makes it harder to fall off your diet at work. Part of your meal planning and shopping will be about what you should eat for lunch. It's much harder to overeat when eating a well-planned lunch.

Going out to lunch every day makes it so easy to go off your diet. Yet, a big part of building work relationships is going out to eat. You still should go out with the gang, but you don't have to go out all the time.

If you need to snack during the day, pack snacks as well. Don't graze from vending machines. They are dangerous. Baby carrots make a great snack. Carrots are filling, low in calories, nutritious, and have a very satisfying crunch when you eat them. When you eat carrots, you feel like you are eating real food. Carrots can also easily be eaten in the car and aren't messy.

This habit isn't just for work. It applies to your kids' school lunches too.

61. Habit: Don't Eat Late at Night

Eating late at night results in lower energy expenditure and weight gain.

You may have heard late night snacking is a no-no. Unfortunately, we now have proof that it's true.

The reason we shouldn't eat when it's dark is simple: when we eat during the daylight hours, we burn more calories than when we eat late at night, in the dark. It's how our internal clocks control energy balance.

It seems we just aren't built to eat late at night. So if you want to burn more calories and lose weight, eat when it's light.

62. Habit: Don't Stockpile Food

You'll eat it if you have it. Eliminate temptation by only buying as much food as you need.

Let's say the store had a sale on chips, so you bought five bags. It was a great deal you couldn't pass up. Will you eat more chips because you bought more?

Yes! Studies show **the more of a particular food you have on hand, the more you will eat.** It's an unconscious process.

You don't know it's happening, and it doesn't make logical sense, but it makes a sort of body sense. When food is available, you eat it, so having a larger food supply may unconsciously encourage larger portions. And, of course, buying treats in bulk and keeping a large cache of sweets around is like a beacon, broadcasting to your brain saying, "come eat me."

How might you combat this threat? **Buy only as much food as you need and no more.** Buying food in bulk may seem like a deal from a money perspective, but the extra weight has its own cost too, and may not be such a bargain when you consider the additional insurance and medical expenses.

63. Habit: Stock Good Food in Vending Machines

Put healthy food alternatives in the vending machine, so people have a choice.

When hunger hit at work, I would walk to the vending machine, and all there was to choose from was junk. I was hungry, so I ate junk. Fellow workers and I often complained about how there was never anything good to eat in the machine. Then we would insert money and buy the junk anyway.

We should have done something about it, but what? I had no idea, so the easiest thing to do was to do nothing. Now I would go the extra step and do something. One extra candy bar a day at work packs on over 20 extra pounds a year. I would try and find out who is in charge of the vending machines and see if I could get them to include healthier alternatives. Even something as simple as switching to baked pretzels from fried chips could make a difference.

Companies interested in health care costs should make good food choices in their vending machines. Unlike schools, getting rid of vending machines at work is impossible, but they can be made healthier. And healthier impacts the bottom line with lower health care costs.

64. Habit: Make Stairways Clean and Safe

Increase the number of steps you take during the day by skipping the elevator and taking the stairs.

One of the big reasons people take the elevator and skip the stairs is they often look like the set of a horror movie.

To make it easy for people to take the stairs, consider the following:

- **Display clear signage pointing to the stairway.** In a lot of buildings, it's hard even to find the stairs.
- **Bring up using the stairs in company-wide memos,** so people know it's an option. It's all about marketing.

- **Make sure the stairway is clean, well-lit, and safe.** A lot of stairways are downright scary. And if they aren't scary, they are so dirty and unpleasant that nobody would use them.
- **Make the stairway environment more pleasant through music and art.** More attractive stairways might encourage people to give them a second look.

Try creating a stairway environment where people want to be, not just a place where they think they should be.

65. Habit: Create Walking School Buses

Instead of taking the bus or cars, parents walk with their kids to school.

In grade school and college, I rode my bike to school. In 1969, 50% of all children walked to school. Today people are understandably worried about the safety of their kids, so riding or walking may not always be an option. Only 25% of kids who live a mile or less from school regularly walk to school.

To revive the ancient and healthy art of walking to school, a group in England started what is called the Walking School Bus. A walking school bus is a group of children who walk to school with one or more adults instead of taking the bus. A fun variation is riding bikes instead of walking.

The simple idea is taking off. It's good for the parents and good for the kids.

Conclusion

We've come a long way together in this book. A lot of ideas have been presented, and I hope you'll take away something valuable. I want to thank you for sticking with me to the end.

Some people ask me how I feel now that I've solved all my weight problems. I have to laugh when I hear that question. My weight problems will never be completely solved. Controlling my weight will always be a struggle. What is different now is that when I start gaining weight, I'll notice before it's too late, and I'll be able to do something about it before my weight spirals out of control.

I may not have solved all my weight problems, but I no longer fear my weight either. I feel like I am back in control. And I like that feeling.

You may feel like you'll never be in control of your weight again, but that's not true. It's never too late. You can take control. I am just like you, and I have learned to control my weight, not by being strong, but by creating a powerful system of weight control habits. I know you can do it too.

Please Review

Feedback is a gift. If you found this book helpful, please review it on Amazon. I appreciate it. It makes all the difference. Thanks!

Please Discuss

I've created a discussion group on *reddit* called, surprisingly, Habit Driven Weight Loss. If you'd like to ask questions or talk more about controlling your weight with habits, please drop by.

Max Workout App—It's Free for You

A major theme in this book is developing exercise as a habit. To help support my exercise habit, I've created an iOS app called *Max Workout*.

Max Workout is designed to help you live a longer and healthier life. How? It trains you to become aerobically fit; to get stronger; to sleep better; and manage your stress.

Get these right, and you can extend your health span, reduce your biological age, and see a 5x reduction in all-cause mortality.

Because you were so kind as to buy this book, I'm giving you one **free year** of access to Max Workout.

To get Max Workout free for one year, follow this Max Workout link on your iPhone or iPad.

The link will take you through the whole download process. Unfortunately, Apple offers can't last forever, so if the link doesn't work for you, please email me at todd@possibility.com, and I'll send you an updated link.

Why did I make a workout app?

Simple, for the rest of my life, I absolutely must work out to control my diabetes and my weight. According to the *Daily Check-in* habit, I need to figure out how to achieve that goal.

First, I researched exercise equipment and found an elliptical machine would work best for me. It's easier on my knees than other options. So, I bought one and put it in our garage.

Now I have a problem; I have to use the dang thing. How do I make that happen?

By making it fun and easy. That's one of the habits too.

I designed Max Workout to make it fun and easy to do all sorts of complex HIIT, reHIT, and Zone 2 cardio routines on my elliptical machine. It also offers many bodyweight strength workout videos. If you want to learn more about what all those abbreviations mean, please visit my website at http://maxapps.info.

Here are a few screenshots to show you what Max Workout looks like.

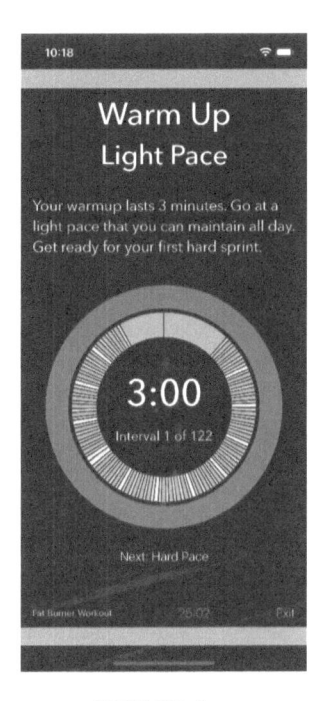

HIIT Workout

Bodyweight Strength Video Workout

Max Workout also has a wide variety of different meditations.

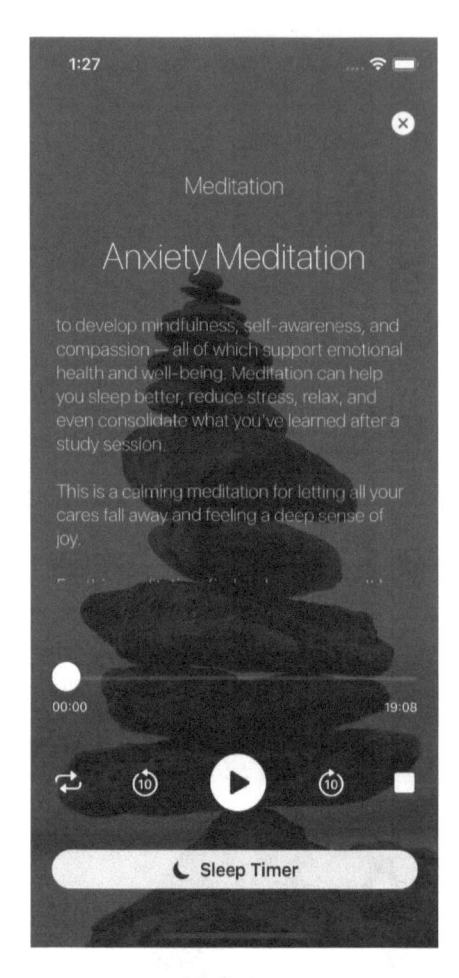

Meditation

Max Workout also helps you sleep better.

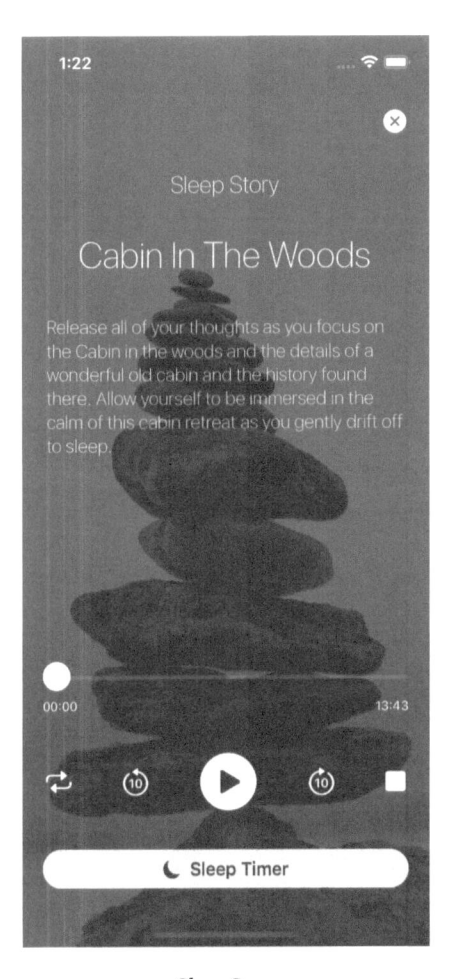

Sleep Story

It works. Max Workout has become a habit for me. I exercise much more regularly and intensely than I would otherwise. And that's the sign of a great habit.

To get Max Workout free for one year, follow this Max Workout link on your iPhone or iPad.

Thanks!

Made in United States
Troutdale, OR
02/09/2025